BUILDING AN ORTHODOX MARRIAGE

*A Practical Commentary on
the Eastern Orthodox Marriage Rite*

T0339171

Building an Orthodox Marriage

A Practical Commentary on the Eastern Orthodox Marriage Rite

BISHOP JOHN (ABDALAH)
of Worcester and New England

NICHOLAS G. MAMEY

ST VLADIMIR'S SEMINARY PRESS
YONKERS, NY 10707
2017

Library of Congress Cataloging-in-Publication Data

Names: Abdalah, John, Bishop of Worcester and New England, author. |
Mamey, Nicholas G., author.
Title: Building an Orthodox marriage : a practical commentary on the Eastern
Orthodox marriage rite / by Bishop John (Abdalah) of Worcester and New
Enland and Nicholas G. Mamey, M.Div., Th.M.
Description: Yonkers, NY : St Vladimirs Seminary Press, [2017] | Includes
bibliographical references. | Description based on print version record and
CIP data provided by publisher; resource not viewed.
Identifiers: LCCN 2017017876 (print) | LCCN 2017020727 (ebook)
| ISBN 9780881415940 | ISBN 9780881415933 (alk. paper) | ISBN
9780881415940 (electronic)
Subjects: LCSH: Marriage—Religious aspects—Orthodox Eastern Church. |
Marriage service—Liturgy.
Classification: LCC BX378.M2 (ebook) | LCC BX378.M2 A333 2017 (print)
| DDC 264/.019085—dc23
LC record available at https://lccn.loc.gov/2017017876

COPYRIGHT © 2017
ST VLADIMIR'S SEMINARY PRESS
575 Scarsdale Rd, Yonkers, NY 10707
1–800–204–2665
www.svspress.com

ISBN 978–0-88141–593–3 (paper)
ISBN 978–0-88141–594–0 (electronic)

PRINTED IN THE UNITED STATES OF AMERICA

Dedicated to

Joanne Josephs Abdalah, Christina Randol Mamey,

and Juliana and Fr Alexander Schmemann,

without whom this work would have been impossible

Contents

Preface

This book is a collaborative effort between Bishop John (Abdalah) of Worcester and New England and Nicholas Mamey, M.Div., Th.M. Completed in 2016, this book presents a practical guide to marriage by exploring the marriage rite of the Eastern Orthodox Church. Bishop John is a widower who married Joanne Josephs in 1978 and rejoiced in their marriage for thirty years before her repose. While working on the book, Nicholas Mamey was engaged to marry Christina Randol (they are now newlyweds). This book is very much a conversation about marriage between these two churchmen, offering a lively, practical, and thoughtful work from two unique perspectives.

This book owes much to the work and life of Fr Alexander Schmemann, who taught generations to pay attention when praying because the theology of the Orthodox Church is well expressed in its ritual and texts. Shortly before his repose, in preparation for a book that he never completed, Fr Alexander taught a single course in 1977 on the liturgical theology of marriage. For the past forty years, Bishop John has been using the materials presented in this course when teaching about marriage. Much of this work was used in Bishop John's dissertation, "Building an Orthodox Marriage," written for his Doctor of Ministry degree from Pittsburgh Theological Seminary. Bishop John and his wife, Joanne, studied pastoral counseling and social work, respectively, and integrated the insights from Orthodox teaching and the social sciences into their pastoral work. Providing more than just academic guidance, Joanne's contribution to this work lay in helping Bishop John to understand the perspective and genius of wives—a gift for which he will forever be grateful.

Nicholas Mamey graduated from Holy Cross Orthodox School of Theology with his Master of Divinity degree in 2014 and Master of Theology in 2016, specializing in Systematic Theology. Engaged to Christina Randol throughout the process of this collaborative work, Nicholas explored the critical, theological, and practical questions that allow for the marrying of theology and everyday life.

This work, which draws upon theology and the social sciences, offers a practical Orthodox guide to living a sanctified married life. In this book the authors present an overview of our Church's perspective on marriage, followed by a detailed commentary on the marriage rite. It is the hope of the authors that this book will be of benefit both to couples preparing to marry and to married couples, by offering wise and practical expressions of our Church's teaching. This book may be used by church groups for marriage enrichment. Those wanting to use this work for marriage preparation in a group setting might find it beneficial to have couples read through Parts One and Two at home, and then work through Part Three as a group. Part Four consists of some practical advice that should be fun for a group to discuss, while the appendix contains some questions that couples should explore before marriage.

The authors offer thanksgiving to God for their brides and for this opportunity to share God's gifts with the readers.

PART I

A Theological Overview

Love: a language, an act of being, a way of thinking, and an approach to life. *Love* is the single word that explains the origin of creation and its meaning for all of us. Love expresses our relationship with God and each other. There is no love outside of God, for "God is love" (1 Jn 4.8). And there is no existence outside of love, because God *Is*.[1] It is through love that we come into being and exist in God and with each other. The fact that we are all created in the image and likeness of a God who works in love and is love shows us that the most natural way that we can live is in love. With this, every human being finds his or her life: to reflect and dwell in the presence of God who poured forth his love unto all of creation.

Each and every one of us is made in the image and likeness of God, and all things have been given to us so that we may live out this fact. This means that the earth, animals, plants, stars, and all of creation, including every person with whom we come into contact, are given to us as a gift from God—so that we may love.[2] This calling,

---

[1] See Exodus 3.14: "God said to Moses, 'I AM WHO I AM.' And he said, 'Say this to the people of Israel, "I AM has sent me to you."'"

[2] Fr Dumitru Staniloe expresses that all creation is a "gift" and discloses to mankind a rational means for coming to know God: "God shows us his love through the world as a gift, so that a progressive dialogue with us in love may come to be." Dumitru Staniloae, *The World: Creation and Deification*, ed. Robert Barringer, trans. Ioan Ioniță, vol. 2 of The Experience of God (Brookline, MA: Holy Cross Orthodox Press, 1994), 7.

this opportunity, this vocation to love is nowhere else more apparent than in the sacrament of marriage, where God gifts a couple with his perfect and peaceful love. This gift to the bride and groom renews, or makes new, a pathway for salvation. Your spouse is united to you so that you may love God in a way that was impossible before.

We Are Liturgical Beings

"So God created man in His own image; in the image of God He created him; male and female He created them" (Gen 1.27). In our very nature, we are blessed by being made in the image and likeness of God himself, as a reflection of the loving work of the Trinity. Mankind was created with such love that God felt it proper to reflect himself in his creation, and with such distinction that all of creation including the angels themselves watched this process in awe.[3] God is revealed both in word and in action as a communal and loving being. Therefore, coming from the Father, the Son, and the Holy Spirit, the proclamation "Let us make man in our image" expresses the fact that man is created to reflect God and become a communal being.[4] Because we are made in the image and likeness of

[3]It is important to note here that the angels themselves did not help God in creating man; rather, the angels became spectators of this miraculous event along with the other creative actions of God himself after their creation. The witness of the angelic hosts and their excitement at the creative process is made evident in Job 38.4–7: "Where wast thou when I laid the foundations of the earth? declare, if thou hast understanding. Who hath laid the measures thereof, if thou knowest? Or who hath stretched the line upon it? Whereupon are the foundations thereof fastened? or who laid the corner stone thereof; when the morning stars sang together, and all the sons of God shouted for joy?" Within this passage it is made clear that the "sons of God" who "shouted for joy" are the angels themselves, who were created before this process. In fact, the book of Job uses this phrase "sons of God" at other times to refer to the angels. See also Job 1.6 and Job 2.1.

[4]See Augustine of Hippo, *On the Holy Trinity* 7.6 (NPNF[1] 3:113): "Both *let us make* and *our* is said in the plural, and ought not to be received except as of relatives. For it was not that gods might make, or make after the image and likeness of gods; but that the Father, and Son, and Holy Spirit might make after the image of

God who created us, it is only appropriate that love towards God is shown forth as obedience: acting in a manner that is complementary to creation, that is, in actions of love and spoken truth. Any other form of human life would simply be unnatural or inhuman, a type of chaos contradicting the divine intention for man. In the words of Fr Alexander Schmemann:

> This response is total obedience in love; not obedience *and* love, but the wholeness of the one as the totality of the other. Obedience, taken in itself, is not a "virtue"; it is blind submission and there is no light in blindness. Only love for God, the absolute object of all love, frees obedience from blindness and makes it the joyful acceptance of that alone which is worthy of being accepted. . . . True obedience is thus true love for God, the true response of Creation to its Creator. Humanity is fully humanity when it is this response to God, when it becomes the movement of total self-giving and obedience to Him.[5]

We are not self-sufficient; rather, we are made to be in relationships. These relationships need God's love to envelop us communally, which is accomplished through Christ by the Holy Spirit. This experience is found in obedience to God and is expressed in man's trust in God. A good God would only will and do that which is good and right for all. Our first relationship is with God and is not reducible to constructs or thoughts. Rather, we understand the relationship between God and us as a personal relationship. We are personal beings made to reflect our Creator. Both personally and communally, we progressively come to understand the incomprehensible God through a dynamic relationship that produces a living

the Father, and Son, and Holy Spirit, that man might subsist as the image of God. And God is the Trinity."

[5]Alexander Schmemann, *For the Life of the World: Sacraments and Orthodoxy* (Crestwood, NY: St Vladimir's Seminary Press, 1973), 84–85.

experience with him. This living experience molds our thoughts, words, and actions, and encompasses the entire person. The perfect expression of this living experience is found within the sacramental services (baptism, the Eucharist, marriage, and all sacramental life). In them, we actively and communally participate in God and become united with him.

It is natural for us to progress in life in a liturgical way; from the time of Adam, liturgical standards were placed in order for us to grow in God. From the start, God told Adam how to live in the garden and how to live with Eve: "Then God blessed them, and God said to them, 'Be fruitful and multiply; fill the earth and subdue it; have dominion over the fish of the sea, over the birds of the air, and over every living thing that moves on the earth'" (Gen 1.28). God has instructed us to take care of everything for his glory. In this ordination (or ordering), we are instructed to cultivate and preserve the gifts given us for the glory of God. In the words of St John of Damascus:

> He made him a sort of miniature world within the larger one, another adoring angel, a compound, an eye-witness of the visible creation, an initiate of the invisible creation, lord of the things of earth, lorded over from on high, earthly and heavenly, passing and immortal, visible and spiritual, halfway between greatness and lowliness, at once spirit and flesh . . . the first that he might endure and give glory to his Benefactor, and the second that he might suffer and by suffering be reminded and instructed not to glory in his greatness.[6]

In receiving the gifts of God and willingly offering them back to him, we are blessed to participate in both heaven and earth, in a

---

[6]John of Damascus, "Orthodox Faith: On Man," in *Saint John of Damascus: Writings*, trans. Frederic Henry Chase, Jr., The Fathers of the Church: A New Translation 37 (Washington, DC: Catholic University of America Press, 1958), 235.

mode of ordered liturgical existence.[7] In this way, we are ourselves offered up in order to perform liturgy, by preserving and participating in all that is "good" (Gen 1.31). "It is *this world* (and not any 'other world'), it is *this life* (and not some 'other life') that were given to man to be a sacrament of the divine presence, given as communion with God, and it is only through this world, this life, by 'transforming' them into communion with God that man *was to be*."[8] With these words Fr Schmemann expressed that this world is not merely a dwelling place for humanity, but an integral part of humanity's aspiration towards transfiguration. Man receives both *"this world"* and *"this life"* to be offered up and transfigured. In this way, mankind may truly become human. This offering of one's self and the world is the purpose of mankind, which is fully realized and expressed in the incarnation of the Word of God himself.

Having become incarnate, the Lord confirmed that creation is good. God created the material world, which he sanctified by his incarnation, death, and resurrection. The intimate connection between the divine and the created (as seen in the creation account of Genesis) is made manifest by Christ's work. Man, created to crown and bless the world in Christ, is called[9] to act in faith. In this act of faith, man celebrates liturgy. Again, in Fr Schmemann's own words:

> In the experience of the Orthodox Church, liturgy is always the *expression* of the faith, life, and teachings of the Church, and, therefore, a sure path to learning these. *"Lex orandi lex est credendi."* "The rule of prayer is the rule of belief." And only insofar

[7]This reception and transfiguration of those things that are received is best illustrated within the Divine Liturgy, in which the holy gifts are offered to God with the words: "Thine own of thine own, in behalf of all and for all."

[8]Schmemann, *Life of the World*, 100. Italics in original.

[9]See Gen 1.28, "And God blessed them, and God said to them, 'Be fruitful and multiply, and fill the earth and subdue it; and have dominion over the fish of the sea and over the birds of the air and over every living thing that moves upon the earth.'"

as we return to this rule, can we recover the true foundations of the Orthodox Christian Education.[10]

Because liturgy is the manifested expression of God and man's action in the Church, a study of the rite of marriage offers an understanding of marriage. This action integrates one into *leitourgia* (λειτουργία), or *liturgy*. *Leitourgia* means more than worship; it signifies the very work and life of the Church.[11] Liturgy is not limited to eucharistic celebrations, but refers to all of the liturgical gatherings of the Church community. When we participate in liturgy, we experience the very life of the Church,[12] and liturgical acts are a participation in the Kingdom of God, which is made possible when two or more are gathered in his name (see Mt 18.20). As Fr Schmemann writes elsewhere: "It is impossible to enter into the spirit of liturgy, to understand its meaning and truly to participate in it without first understanding that it is built primarily on the double rhythm of *preparation* and *fulfillment*, and that this rhythm is essential to the Church's liturgy because it reveals and indeed fulfills the double nature and function of the Church herself."[13]

We are liturgical beings.[14] As such, we are called to gather together and *work* in a relationship with God, not as individuals, but as the Body of Christ, the Church. As the Church, we join together in the

---

[10]Alexander Schmemann, *Liturgy and Life: Lectures and Essays on Christian Development through Liturgical Experience* (New York, NY: Department of Religious Education of the Orthodox Church in America, 1974), 22.

[11]This word in Greek literally means "common work" or "common action," which aptly describes the way we participate in worship.

[12]See Schmemann, *Liturgy*, 23.

[13]Alexander Schmemann, *Of Water and the Spirit: A Liturgical Study of Baptism* (Crestwood, NY: St Vladimir's Seminary Press, 1974), 16.

[14]See John Zizioulas, "On Creation, Salvation, Christology and Ecclesiology," in *Lessons on Christian Dogmatics* (Thessaloniki: Publication Services, 2005). During this lecture series Zizoulas argues that "man has to become a liturgical being before he can hope to overcome his ecological crisis." Becoming a "liturgical being" is, in its very nature, a process.

ongoing life, love, and work of the Trinity by offering all things and praise to God. Because we are joined to Christ in baptism, the work we do is done in Christ and through Christ, which brings us all to the Father by the Holy Spirit. We do this work so that we may reflect Christ and his priestly example of praising the Father and caring for man. The care and service to all people lovingly shown by the Church is expressed through her services and in all of the time between services. A beautiful and full expression of this is found in the service of husband and wife to each other, who share their God-given gift of love. This love procreates, and offers an image of oneness like that of the Holy Trinity. This love is reflective of the God who created us, for God creates and mankind procreates. This love puts the needs and desires of the other before one's own for the sake of salvation. It is always holy, patient, and kind, ever reflecting the person of God.

Interacting with other persons constitutes a vital aspect not only of performing liturgy, but also of being human. The marriage rite as a liturgy and sacrament is no exception to the communal and participatory experience of God. In participating we become fulfilled, yet in being fulfilled, we become even more ready to participate. The experience we have with the eternal and unconstrained God is potentially precisely that: eternal and unconstrained. Because we are intended to live liturgically toward the communal God, the "other" becomes necessary for us to become fully human.

"It is not good for man to be alone."

Because we are made in the image and likeness of a communal and perfect God, the most natural way in which we can live is in community. Our very nature is relational, which reflects who God is. As mentioned before, "God is love" (1 Jn 4.8), and this Love is perfectly and communally shared between the Son and the Spirit, pouring out unto all of mankind. We experience each other as gifts in community, which allows us to complete our nature as persons who can, like God, love. Without each other, we would be alone and unable to love; "It is not good for man to be alone" (Gen 2.18). In the book of Genesis, gives Adam a solution for his solitude, providing him companionship with the bringing forth of Eve. With this gift, man is no longer alone. God willed and created a partner to be in relationship with man, derived from man and sustained by God.[15]

In bringing forth each of them, God presents Adam and Eve to each other, granting them each the opportunity to love one another. Because the other is the image and likeness of God, loving the other allows each to love God, whom they experience in each other. In marriage, you become united with the other (your spouse), reflecting the love and unity that God shares with you. Our relationship to God is one of obedience. Likewise, in marriage both spouses submit to God and obey God. The other leads us to God: we obey and submit to each other because this helps us submit to and obey God. Submission in marriage is about following God's will, and not about one spouse's domination over the other. The head of the house is Christ, because he is the one who gives marriage, and it is the responsibility of both husband and wife to receive God's direction and save the other. In the wedding service we read from Ephesians 5.21, "Be subject to one another in reverence to Christ." Again, in obedient love, God is encountered through the spouse. In the words of Archdeacon John Chryssavgis, "The other person in marriage, the marriage partner, is the life-giving personal revelation of Christ."[16] It is in their united desire to serve God through each other that the husband and wife grow more intensely united as one. Such a love for

---

[15]See Gen 2.21: "And the LORD God caused a deep sleep to fall on Adam, and he slept; and He took one of his ribs, and closed up the flesh in its place."

[16]John Chryssavgis, *Love, Sexuality, and the Sacrament of Marriage* (Brookline, MA: Holy Cross Orthodox Press, 1996), 17.

the other, when placed in the hands of God, has no bounds; rather, it has infinite potential and is written in eternity. From the pen of Fr John Meyendorff:

> St. Paul affirms that marriage also has a place in the eternal Kingdom. The husband becomes one single being, one single "flesh" with his wife, just as the Son of God ceased to be only Himself, i.e., God, and became *also* man so that the community of His people may also become His Body. This is why, so often, the Gospel narratives compare the Kingdom of God with a wedding feast, which fulfills the Old Testament prophetic visions of a wedding between God and Israel, the elected people. And this is also why a truly Christian marriage can only be unique, not in virtue of some abstract law or ethical precept but precisely because it is a Mystery of the Kingdom of God introducing man into *eternal* joy and *eternal* love.[17]

Oneness in God by means of marriage to another is not static, but rather is an organic, ever-changing state, the goal of which is to grow together in oneness by moving towards God through each other. This oneness is realized in the uniting of husband and wife in God. This is made clear when Jesus said, "But from the beginning of the creation, God 'made them male and female.' 'For this reason a man shall leave his father and mother and be joined to his wife, and the two shall become one flesh'; so then they are no longer two, but one flesh" (Mk 10.6–8). The husband lives for the wife and the wife for the husband, serving each other as they would the Lord. Just as the Word subjected his human will to that of the Father, in marriage we subjugate our will to that of God through our spouse. This sacrifice is a reflection of the ultimate offering of Christ on the cross, a pain overshadowed by the tremendous joy that comes from it.

[17]John Meyendorff, *Marriage: An Orthodox Perspective* (Crestwood, NY: St Vladimir's Seminary Press, 1975), 19–20.

As you become completely *one* with your spouse, it is undeniable that marriage consists in living united in Christ by means of being completely vulnerable and open to each other. The love attainable in marriage approaches the infinite, and yet is always developing. This united life gives you the potential to better "know" your spouse in ways impossible by any other means. "Know" in this context coveys an intimacy that is far greater than intellectual sharing. Marriage offers a constant sharing of life, including all of our worst and most honest moments. Husbands and wives share visions, dreams, hopes, beds, food, and nearly every aspect of their lives. Sharing in this sacramental life allows for a unique bond with only one other, having as its uniting force the infinite God of perfect unity. There is an eternal reality of unbreakable oneness with the other in the sacrament of marriage that is endangered only by estrangement and resistance to serve God with and through the other.[18]

The sacrament of marriage is an expression and actual experience of God's gift of love, of the grace that flows among the three persons of the Trinity even before time and the calling of creation into being. Therefore, love is timeless and eternal. In the marriage service God is called to send down his perfect love upon this couple: "That He will send down upon them perfect and peaceful love, and assistance."[19] God gives the couple perfect and peaceful love; they in turn are called to reflect in their life together the love that exists between the members of the Trinity and the love between Christ and his Church.

---

[18]See Augustine of Hippo, *On Marriage and Concupiscence* 1.19 (NPNF[1] 5:271). "The sacramental bond, again, which is lost neither by divorce nor by adultery, should be guarded by husband and wife with concord and chastity. For it alone is that which even an unfruitful marriage retains by the law of piety, now that all that hope of fruitfulness is lost for the purpose of which the couple married."

[19]Betrothal Service, Great Litany. Quotations of the marriage service are taken from *The Sacrament of Holy Matrimony,* with commentary by V. Rev. John Meyendorff (New York, NY: Department of Religious Education of the Orthodox Church in America, 2009), sometimes with minor alterations.

This model of love is reflected in the Epistle reading prescribed for the wedding service. In Ephesians 5.20–33, St Paul speaks of the relationship between Christ and his Church, using the relationship of husband and wife as an illustration. We read in that passage how the husband cares for the wife and her every need in the same way that he cares for his own body. He loves her enough to die for her, while she completes him, reverences him, and cares for him. Likewise, he loves and cherishes her, completes her, cares for her, and shares God with her. God creates us male and female with the capacity to relate to each other and reflect God in our love for each other. When we recognize that God is acting in our lives, we become open to developing the skills of communicating with trust, faith, and love. Such oneness allows marriage to be fruitful, rewarding, and uniting. As we learn to communicate better, our marriages progress, deepening in oneness. It is in this manner of living in community, like that of the Trinity, that love brings us into a deeper knowledge of each other and God.

In this model, there is little room for "self-righteousness" or selfishness. In fact, there is no such thing. "Self-righteousness" becomes nothing more than an oxymoron, because only God is righteous and is perfect community as three persons. True righteousness is of God and cannot be experienced when one is confined merely to the self. Righteousness is experienced when we love our spouse, and God completes this love for the purpose of salvation in him. It is unfortunate that some couples, because of fear or immaturity, hide from each other and never actualize their potential. Such instances lead to isolation and are unnatural, inhuman, and do not at all constitute unity.

Marriage is a way of life that leads to salvation, because as we, as husbands and wives, approach each other in sacrifice and love, we approach Christ himself. Again in the words of Fr Schmemann,

"Christ, the Divine Love Himself, stands in the midst of us, transforming our mutual alienation into brotherhood. As I advance towards the other, as the other comes to me—we begin to realize that it is Christ Who brings us together by His love for both of us."[20] The blessing of God himself to us, as man and woman in marriage, gives us an opportunity to abolish our former isolation. In all persons, whether married or not, there is the natural need to love the other; this is a crucial truth and the basis of our human nature. We are developing beings. It is in the process of sacrificial communion with those other than ourselves, and only in this process, that we experience righteousness and dwell in the presence of Christ. By becoming humble servants of one another, we as husbands and wives reflect the righteousness of Christ, who humbled himself for the life of the world. In understanding the other in God, by love and sacrifice, husbands and wives come to know and experience the life of Christ.

Coming to Know Christ as Light in Both Marriage and Life

Marriage in the Church is a revolutionary experience of love; revolutionary, not because two individuals have come together, but because the love experienced by these two persons is unlike that which the world has ever seen. Because of the incarnation, death, and resurrection of Christ, husbands and wives in Christ can achieve that which the fallen world cannot offer. In Christ, that which is divided is united, and that which is broken is restored. With Christ's own grace, divine love is given to those whom God has united at his own heavenly altar. Husbands and wives are united to Christ and each other, and while still in this world, they belong to God's

---

[20]A reflection on Forgiveness Sunday given by Fr Alexander Schmemann of blessed memory. Alexander Schmemann, "Protopresbyter Alexander Schmemann: Forgiveness Sunday," accessed March 10, 2017, http://www.schmemann.org/byhim/forgivenesssunday.html.

kingdom. Christ has allowed mankind to experience an unbounded love, which transcends the mundane activity of this life and invites mankind into eternity. God is Love, and by his action, the love of husband and wife is revolutionary.

In the words of King David in Psalm 143, "Cause me to hear Your lovingkindness in the morning, For in You do I trust; Cause me to know the way in which I should walk, For I lift up my soul to You." As one learns to trust in God, God responds by revealing our selves to us. This is done progressively and slowly so that the depth of one's soul may not be traumatized, and so that the relationship between divine and human can endure. Husband and wife continue to grow in true knowledge by allowing God to correct the things that prevent them from living in accordance with their true nature. It is a completely communal process, leaving no room for isolation. In the words of St Macarius, "It is of no use for the heavenly places; it is of no use for the kingdom—that soul which supposes that it can achieve perfect purity of itself, and by itself alone, without the Spirit."[21] In coming to know Truth in God, one experiences light; this is the relationship between knowing and spiritual purity. Both of these require complete reliance on God.

"In Him was life, and the life was the light of men" (Jn 1.4). Jesus Christ gave clarity and truth to the world by living, dying, and rising for it. Christ has life in himself, and when John states that this "*life was the light of men*," he gives a new meaning to the word "light." "Light" is the perfect commingling between the knowledge of truth and purity within a person; it is a metaphor for the relationship between knowledge and holy action.[22] The "light of man" is an

---

[21]Macarius the Great, "Homily 24," in *Fifty Spiritual Homilies of St. Macarius the Egyptian*, trans. Arthur James Mason, Translations of Christian Literature Series I: Greek Text (London: Society For Promoting Christian Knowledge, 1921), 176.

[22]"φῶς [*phōs*, Eng. 'light'] is used to denote truth and its knowledge, together with the spiritual purity congruous with it." Joseph Henry Thayer, trans., rev., and

expression of the state wherein mankind is both called to dwell and able to find life—in Christ. In coming to know and serve Christ, the eternal Truth, one experiences light; one is given life.

In marriage, we participate in the mystery of our spouse. The deeper we journey together in oneness, the more the mystery of Christ is revealed through the spouse. It is in this relationship based on faith in Christ that married persons mystically unite with each other and with Christ, and husband and wife discover Christ and each other in this process. Faith in Christ and unity with one's spouse transform the individual into a person in relationship with God and the other. Having partaken in the divine and holy mystery of marriage, we are mystically and completely united with each other. "Have you not read that He who made them at the beginning 'made them male and female,' and said, 'For this reason a man shall leave his father and mother and be joined to his wife, and the two shall become one flesh'? So they are no longer two but one flesh" (Mt 19.4b–6). By trusting in God and having become united with the other, one is called to serve God by showing one's spouse sacrificial love.

Marriage is a gift of love, involving a union of pathways for the purpose of working out our salvation. When we marry, each of us maintains our distinct personhood while being one with each other. This relationship is maintained in the kingdom of heaven in the same way that other relationships, such as that of parent and child, are. Together the two individuals, who are mystically one, begin to know God through the other in ways that before marriage were impossible for the individual. Now one, the married couple as male and female take up their new lives in God's light. From this time, with eternal promises and God-given gifts, we take up our distinctive roles

enl., C. L. Wilibald Grimm, and C. G. Wilke, *A Greek-English Lexicon of the New Testament: Being Grimm's Wilke's Clavis Novi Testamenti*, 4th ed. (1901; repr., Grand Rapids, MI: Baker Book House, 1977), s.v. "STRONGS NT 5457: φῶς."

within marriage. Obedience and light are beautifully articulated by Fr Schmemann in his book *For the Life of the World*:

> [I]n the "natural" world the bearer of this obedient love, of this love as response, is the woman. The man proposes, the woman accepts. This acceptance is not passivity, blind submission, because it is love, and love is always active. It gives life to the proposal of man, fulfills it as life, yet it becomes fully love and fully life only when it is fully *acceptance* and *response*. This is why the whole creation, the whole Church—and not only women—find the expression of their response and obedience to God in Mary the Woman, and rejoice in her. She stands for all of us, because only when we accept, respond in love and obedience—only when we accept the essential womanhood of creation—do we become ourselves true men and women; only then can we indeed *transcend* our limitations as "males" and "females." For man can be truly man—that is, the king of creation, the priest and minister of God's creativity and initiative—only when he does not posit himself as the "owner" of creation and submits himself—in obedience and love—to its nature as the bride of God, in *response* and *acceptance*. And woman ceases to be just a "female" when, totally and unconditionally accepting the life of the Other as *her own life*, giving herself totally to the Other, she becomes the very expression, the very fruit, the very joy, the very beauty, the very gift of our response to God, the one whom, in the words of the song, the king will bring into his chambers, saying: "Thou art all fair, my love, there is no spot in thee" (Song 4.7).[23]

---

[23]Schmemann, *Life of the World*, 85.

Relationship before Marriage

The Church understands the complexities of our lives. Particularly in the sacraments the Church meets us where we are. The Church acknowledges our complex relationships, problems, accomplishments, drama, and every other aspect of our lives. In fact, one of the functions of the Church is to bring clarity to our lives; to transfigure them, and facilitate our journey towards good. The Church and those therein mourn with us, rejoice with us, and suffer with us. "Rejoice with those who rejoice, and weep with those who weep. Be of the same mind toward one another. Do not set your mind on high things, but associate with the humble. Do not be wise in your own opinion" (Rom 12.15–16). The Church does not ignore the relationship that has already developed between bride and bridegroom. Our tradition embraces this relationship before marriage as one that is already in the process of growing in oneness. We couples begin to complete each other's sentences as we share our lives and perspectives. Already while courting we are sharing time, dreams, and hopes. Together we respond to the challenges in each other's lives as well as our common challenges as a couple. This causes us to share an experience of God and the world, which we hold in common. The problems that we face and the solutions of such problems cause us to accommodate new information and develop new problem-solving skills. It changes our very experience of the world. When we share life, we build common and united understandings, perspectives, and desires.

This comes at a great cost to our families of origin.[24] We will not only surprise them with changed hearts and minds, but we will leave them frightened, not knowing how the roles we played in our families of origin will be fulfilled, how our spouse will or won't be integrated, and how the members of our family of origin will

[24]"Family of origin" refers to the family one grew up in.

respond to our changed minds. This fear will probably not subside until the families of origin experience the bride and groom's continued participation in the family of origin, while ensuring the needs of the family members are met. For most families, this process is quite painful and dramatic. Marriage causes families of origin to be redesigned. It would serve all well to be patient with each other, understanding that everyone needs to grow and change to make room for the sacramental union we are anticipating. Flexibility from all family members will serve to lessen the pain of the perceived extraction. Two former family members are taken from their family of origin to be united as a new family. This is of course only until the new family reconnects with the family of origin as an extended and unified family. It helps to understand that the extracted members will come back, but they will return as adults, and the extended family will find new ways of meeting daily needs. Some families lack the necessary flexibility to let one member go to form a new family. Marriage is a gift that brings new life, but all change is difficult and frightening. In such cases the parish community can be a valuable support in helping reassure all that God and his Church will not abandon them in this transitional time.

PART II

Definitions

The Time, or *Kairos*,[1] of the Sacramental Marriage

Sacraments (such as marriage) cannot be reduced to momentary acts in history. Sacraments are God acting with us and impact our lives before and after the gift. "For a 'sacrament' . . . implies necessarily the idea of transformation, refers to the ultimate event of Christ's death and resurrection, and is always a sacrament of the Kingdom."[2] Just as the marriage impacts our families of origin, it impacts our individual lives before and after the liturgical service. God blesses us as we date, and he allows our love and intimacy to grow throughout our lives and, perhaps, into his kingdom. This is further expressed within the patristic writings of the Church. Marriage is understood to be a unique and eternal act that is a holy gift.[3] Although this service is a single act, the Church too under-

---

[1]*Kairos* (καιρός) is a Greek word for a special or opportune time. In the Church we often use it to mean "God's time." In liturgy we enter into God's time, which is outside of historical time and is in eternity.

[2]Schmemann, *Life of the World*, 81.

[3]"For the laying down of the law of once marrying, the very origin of the human race is our authority; witnessing as it emphatically does what God constituted in the beginning for a type to be examined with care by posterity. For when He had moulded man, and had foreseen that a peer was necessary for him, He borrowed from his ribs one, and fashioned for him one woman; whereas, of course, neither the Artificer nor the material would have been insufficient (for the creation of more). There were more ribs in Adam, and hands that knew no weariness in God; but not

stands this sacrament not to be bound by time and to be communal by involving the whole community in its action.

In a way, of course, the whole life of the Church can be termed sacramental, for it is always the manifestation in time of the "new time." Yet in a more precise way the Church calls sacraments those decisive acts of its life in which this transforming grace is *confirmed as being given*, in which the Church through a liturgical act identifies itself with and becomes the very form of that Gift.[4]

In the prayer of the betrothal, we ask God to "confirm the word which they have spoken." This "word" is not in reference to anything said by the bride or the groom in the ceremony, nor is it a reference to a previous ceremony. Rather, according to Fr Schmemann, this "word" refers to the dreams and discussions expressed during their courting period.[5] The idea that marriage is dynamic and extends from the wedding service in both directions, both before and after, is expressed liturgically by the resistance of the Church to pronounce a couple "*now* husband and wife." We would also acknowledge that a couple who has spent fifty years together has shared more and is more united than that same couple was on their wedding day. This further emphasizes that the relationship created in marriage is eternal and dynamic.

Outside the Church, marriage is generally understood as a legal contract, necessary for the stability of a society that needs to manage

more wives in the eye of God. And accordingly the man of God, Adam, and the woman of God, Eve, discharging mutually (the duties of) one marriage, sanctioned for mankind a type by (the considerations of) the authoritative precedent of their origin and the primal will of God. Finally, 'there shall be,' said He, 'two in one flesh,' not three nor four." Tertullian, *On Exhortation to Chastity* 5 (ANF 4:53).

[4]Schmemann, *Life of the World*, 81.

[5]Alexander Schmemann, "Liturgical Theology of Marriage" (lecture, St Vladimir's Orthodox Theological Seminary, Crestwood, NY, 1977).

estates and account for property holdings. In the fifth chapter of the letter to the Ephesians, we discover a different meaning of Christian marriage, that element which cannot be reduced to either Judaic utilitarianism or Roman legalism—the possibility and the responsibility given to both husband and wife to transfigure their agreement into the reality of the Kingdom.[6] Christian marriage cannot be reduced to contracts and rights, because its intention is to allow persons to reflect God, in whose image they were created, through love. Furthermore, marriage in the Church is not merely permission from the Church to be together, but is the elevation and transformation of the natural inclination of man and woman to be together in love. Fr Schmemann expounds on this point:

> We can now understand that its true meaning is not that it merely gives a religious "sanction" to marriage and family life, reinforces with supernatural grace the natural family virtues. Its meaning is that by taking the "natural" marriage into "the great mystery of Christ and the Church," the sacrament of matrimony gives marriage *a new meaning*; it transforms, in fact, not only marriage as such but all human love. . . . For the Christian, *natural* does not mean either self-sufficient—a "nice little family"—or merely insufficient, and to be, therefore, strengthened and completed by the addition of the "*supernatural.*" The natural man thirsts and hungers for fulfillment and redemption. This thirst and hunger is the *vestibule* of the Kingdom: both beginning and exile.[7]

It is clear that the marriage liturgy is more than a contract; it is a participation in a saving action of God. This blessing confirms that the events, tears, and joys between the betrothed couple have been

---

[6]In Ephesians 5, St Paul instructs husbands to cherish their wives and wives to respect their husbands because the mystery of their marriage parallels that of Christ and the Church.

[7]Schmemann, *Life of the World*, 88–89.

guided by God as sacramentally uniting. What is being done here is not magic, but the culmination and revelation of marital unity. This union is not limited to the relationship between the bride and groom, but applies to the entire community of the Church. Again, Fr Schmemann asserts, "As long as we visualize marriage as the concern of those alone who are being married, as something that happens to them and not to the whole Church, and, therefore, to the world itself, we shall never understand the truly sacramental meaning of marriage. . . ."[8] The Church is invited to witness, pray for, affirm, and accept the marriage, and is called to continue to support the marriage throughout its salvific journey.

Before the crowning service begins, the betrothal service opens with a set of petitions to God, in which the deacon (or the priest), on behalf of the congregation and the couple, asks God to meet every conceivable need of the couple. The *ektenia* (liturgical set of petitions) begins by placing the Church in Christ's "peace," which is in reference to the same Old Testament concept of *shalom* (שָׁלוֹם). We then ask for peace from above, peace for the world, the building up of the churches of God and the local Church community, the strengthening of the bishop and clergy, the health of the couple, and that they might be given a blameless life and steadfastness of faith. We continue by praying for God to deliver the couple from wrath, danger, and necessity.

This service allows us to put aside earthly cares in order to be free to focus on the heavenly and eternal things. However, such will and action to lay aside the worries, anxieties, and bothersome cares of the world are not only prescribed to prevent distraction, but allow for us to be transformed and join the angels who ceaselessly worship God.[9] In doing so, we ready ourselves to receive the eternal Christ.

[8]Ibid., 82.
[9]See Rev 4.8, wherein the cherubim and their form of worship is described:

"Let us who mystically represent the cherubim and sing the thrice-holy hymn to the life-giving Trinity, lay aside all earthly care. . . . That we may receive the King of all who comes invisibly upborne by the angelic hosts."[10] Although this hymn is found in the eucharistic liturgy, all liturgy is cooperation with God's work. Mankind is not only spiritual, but also material. As such it is appropriate that we give our entire selves (soul and body, the spiritual and the material) to God and each other. We relate to each other in both spiritual and material ways. In the words of Met. Kallistos (Ware):

> The supreme purpose of marriage is that husband and wife should help the other to enter the heavenly kingdom. Through their mutual love and their shared life, the two of them—together with their children, if God has given them offspring—are called to bring one another closer to Christ. As an eternal union between two unique and eternal personalities, the sacrament of marriage has no other end than this.[11]

In marriage, husbands and wives teach each other how to communicate, or commune, with each other. While each comes from a respective family system with its own rules of communications, its own interpretations of body language, and its own idiosyncratic word usage, they come together to form a new family and to develop their own family with still another unique system. By making Christ the leader of the new family and making salvation the goal, the new family has a common direction pointed toward God himself. By hearing the gospel together and by responding to sermons and

"... and day and night they never cease to sing, 'Holy, holy, holy, is the Lord God Almighty, who was and is and is to come!'"

[10]The Cherubic Hymn, sung immediately before the Great Entrance in the Divine Liturgy.

[11]Kallistos (Ware), foreword to *Marriage as a Path to Holiness: Lives of Married Saints*, by David Ford and Mary Ford, 2nd ed. (Waymart, PA: St. Tikhon's Monastery Press, 2013), xi.

church educational events, we together forge a common experience and life in Christ. Together and from within the Church, we learn to be a Christian couple, Orthodox parents, and mature empty-nesters. The whole Church community serves to support us, to teach us, and later to be served by us.

Mystery and Symbol

The theology of marriage is reflected in the rite of marriage itself. Like all sacramental services in the Orthodox Church, we understand God to be acting through symbols that allow us to respond to him without being overwhelmed. The holy fathers and teachers of the Church understand marriage to be holy, which means belonging to God, and to be a sacrament, or *mystery*,[12] which means that God is acting through them in our lives. This sacrament reflects the relationship between Christ and the Church and shows that the Church is an expression of marriage, as noted in St Paul's letter to the Ephesians: "This is a great mystery: but I speak concerning Christ and the Church" (Eph 5.23).

The word "sacrament" originates from the Greek word *mystērion* (μυστήριον), which is a derivative of the verb *myō* (μύω), meaning "to close the eyes for the purpose of protecting them from a . . . vision of deity."[13] This definition of "sacrament" paints an icon of dwelling in the presence of God, where the extreme brilliance of God is revealed to the participant(s) for the intention of change.

---

[12]See Augustine of Hippo, *On Marriage and Concupiscence* 1.11 (*NPNF*[1] 5:268): "It is certainly not fecundity only, the fruit of which consists of offspring, nor chastity only, whose bond is fidelity, but also a certain sacramental bond in marriage which is recommended to believers in wedlock." See also ibid., 1.19 (*NPNF*[1] 5:271): "In matrimony, however, let these nuptial blessings be the objects of our love—offspring, fidelity, the sacramental bond."

[13]Nicon D. Patrinacos, *A Dictionary of Greek Orthodoxy: Lexikon Hellenikes Orthodoxias* (Pleasantville, NY: Hellenic Heritage Publications, 1984), 326.

The mystery of marriage and its sacramentality are found in the grace of God, which is granted to the participant for the ability to bear the intense experience and inexplicable transformation of, and participation in, becoming one mind and one flesh with another.[14] Again, Fr Schmemann expresses this understanding well in *For the Life of the World*:

> For a "sacrament," as we have seen, implies necessarily the idea of transformation, refers to the ultimate event of Christ's death and resurrection, and is always a sacrament of the Kingdom. In a way, of course, the whole life of the Church can be termed sacramental, for it is always the manifestation in time of the "new time." Yet in a more precise way the Church calls sacraments those decisive acts of its life in which this transforming grace is *confirmed as being given*, in which the Church through a liturgical act identifies itself with and becomes the very form of that Gift.[15]

God's grace is revealed to us in an earthly form as symbol, allowing us to participate in this heavenly reality. Naturally, we as finite beings feel a need to explain who God is and how he works. This is a task that uses definitions and limited language for the indefinable and infinite. When we attempt to do this, it does not capture the reality itself; rather, this attempt helps make tangible that which is intangible. The Holy Spirit works through words and objects regardless of their flaws and limitations, so that we may return to God and experience the Kingdom in every sense. The liturgical experience

---

[14]In the "Prayers of Thanksgiving After Holy Communion," the communicant prays the following prayer, which shows the ineffability of the gift of being made worthy to receive the body and blood of Christ. "I thank thee, O Lord my God, that thou hast not rejected me, a sinner, but hast accounted me worthy to become a communicant of thy holy Mysteries. I thank thee that thou hast accounted me, the unworthy, worthy to partake of thine immaculate and heavenly gifts."

[15]Schmemann, *Life of the World*, 81.

allows for the invisible to be accessed through the visible, the uncreated through the created, and the immaterial through the material. These material symbols (signs) are mystically transfigured and contain the whole of what they point to, and the sacraments (such as marriage) become eternal through the appropriate reception, use, and intention of these signs.[16] Archdeacon Chryssavgis offers the following:

> Marriage is, according to the Orthodox view, a sacrament because through it God directly reveals the heavenly Kingdom to the world in two specific persons. At each stage of our life, the mystery of salvation becomes a real experience through the various sacraments. . . . In each case, new life enters the human person as a real presence and gift, not as an oblation or magic.[17]

The sacramental understanding of marriage is that God is acting and his grace is revealed through earthly symbols. Each of these symbols is a visible sign of divine grace, which has an inner reality, a heavenly reality in the kingdom of God. The symbols found within the rite of marriage include rings, crowns, the common cup, and the Gospel Book. These symbols are used in order to express the activity of the heavenly in participation with the earthly and to demonstrate how the Church has always connected us to God's work and to his kingdom.

Christians have always understood marriage to be an integral part of life in the Church. St John Chrysostom cites St Ignatius of Antioch (first century) as one who blessed marriage as a state that is

---

[16]Schmemann, *Life of the World*, 141. For Schmemann, a sign is not merely that which points to otherness or a gesture towards reality; rather, the sign is a manifestation of the divine reality experienced. A "sign" is an epiphany that visibly reveals the invisible insofar as the integrity of its ontology is not "dissolved" in the other: "We called this relationship an *epiphany*. 'A *is* B' means that the whole of A expresses, communicates, reveals, manifests the 'reality' of B."

[17]Chryssavgis, *Sacrament of Marriage*, 17.

entered by the blessing of the bishop,[18] whose function it is to discern what is good for the Christian. Marriages should be for the salvation of the faithful, and so cannot be reduced to earthly functions.

Rings

The rings are the first of the truly symbolic items that are shared between the couple preparing for marriage. The rings possess different symbolic meanings, all of which are helpful in understanding the significance of the rings. In having the couple put on the rings during the betrothal service, the Church calls to mind God's pledge to those who follow him. The rings show God's fidelity[19] and call us to respond to his covenant: "I will be your God and you will be my people" (Ex 6.7). The illustrations in the prayer prescribed for the rings invite the bride and groom to participate in and receive this same blessing as their forefathers.[20] Secondly, the rings may also express the joining of two godly persons who become a new household dedicated to God.

The ring is an important symbol in the Old Testament, and this symbolism carries on through the New Testament. Within ancient Jewish culture a ring was considered to not only be a sign of adornment,[21] but, more specifically, a sign of one's commitment. A "signet

---

[18]John Chrysostom, *On Marriage and Family Life*, trans. Catherine P. Roth and David Anderson, Popular Patristics Series 7 (Crestwood, NY: St Vladimir's Seminary Press, 1986), 12. [See St Ignatius' *Epistle to Polycarp* 5.2: "But it is right for men and women who marry to be united with the consent of the bishop, that the marriage be according to the Lord and not according to lust (cf. Tob 8.7)" (Lake, LCL).—*Ed.*]

[19]The word "fidelity" here is not understood as mankind's fidelity towards God, but God's fidelity towards mankind. He keeps every promise and is ever faithful towards his creation. "For the Son of God, Jesus Christ, whom we preached among you, Silvanus and Timothy and I, was not Yes and No; but in him it is always Yes." (2 Cor 1.19)

[20]Meyendorff, *Marriage*, 32.

[21]The Jewish word for "ring," *tabba'ath*, comes from the word *tabah'*, which literally means "sink." This is probably because the ring would sink into the document as it was pressing its seal into it.

ring" bore the imprint of a specific seal, worn by those of high authority;[22] such rings were pressed into wax that sealed important documents or items to indicate authenticity, ownership, and/or approval.[23] There are multiple instances throughout Scripture that refer to the exchange of these rings (i.e., signet rings) between persons. In each of these cases the ring is given to a person who thereby receives a position of honor and authority. Husband and wife freely give themselves to each other, and this special relationship is one of covenant. Authority in marriage refers to the authority over the home that the couple makes together. In the betrothal service the rings are blessed, and the prayer points to rings throughout biblical history:

> PRIEST: O Lord our God, who didst accompany the servant of the patriarch Abraham into Mesopotamia, when he was sent to espouse a wife for his lord Isaac, and who, by means of the drawing of water, didst reveal to him that he should betroth Rebecca: Do Thou, the same Lord, bless also the betrothal of these Thy servants, [*name*] and [*name*], and confirm the promise that they have made. Establish them in the holy union which is from Thee. For in the beginning Thou didst make them male and female, and by Thee the woman is joined unto the man as a helper and for the procreation of the human race. Therefore, O Lord our God, who hast sent forth Thy truth upon Thine inheritance, and

---

[22]See Esth 3.12: "Then the king's scribes were called on the thirteenth day of the first month, and *a decree* was written according to all that Haman commanded—to the king's satraps, to the governors who *were* over each province, to the officials of all people, to every province according to its script, and to every people in their language. In the name of King Ahasuerus it was written, and sealed with the king's signet ring."

[23]See Clement of Alexandria, *The Instructor* 3.11 (*ANF* 2:285). "The Word [Christ], then, permits them [women] a finger-ring of gold. Nor is this for ornament, but for sealing things which are worth keeping safe in the house, in the exercise of their charge of housekeeping."

Thy covenant unto Thy servants our fathers, Thine elect from generation to generation: Look upon Thy servant, [*name*], and Thy handmaiden, [*name*], and establish and make firm their betrothal, in faith and in oneness of mind, in truth and in love. For Thou, O Lord, hast declared that a pledge should be given and confirmed in all things. By a ring power was given to Joseph in Egypt; by a ring Daniel was glorified in the land of Babylon; by a ring the uprightness of Tamar was revealed; by a ring our heavenly Father showed His bounty upon His Son, for He said: Bring the fatted calf and kill it, and let us eat and make merry. By Thine own right hand, O Lord, Thou didst arm Moses in the Red Sea; by Thy true word the heavens were established, and the foundations of the earth were made firm; and the right hands of Thy servants also shall be blessed by Thy mighty word and by Thine upraised arm. Therefore, O Master, bless now this putting-on of rings with Thy heavenly blessing, and let Thine angel go before them all the days of their life. For Thou art He that blesses and sanctifies all things, and unto Thee are due all glory, honor, and worship: to the Father, and to the Son, and to the Holy Spirit, now and ever and unto ages.

By a ring power was given to Joseph in Egypt

Being disturbed by his dreams and in search for a clear answer to their meaning, Pharaoh sent for Joseph, who was dwelling in a dungeon, a lowly place from where he would soon be exalted. When Joseph was brought before the ruler, he prophesied and interpreted the dreams of Pharaoh, thus saving Egypt from famine and death, and Pharaoh did something quite extraordinary. He granted Joseph the authority to rule over his house, and indicated this by giving his signet ring to Joseph.

"You shall be over my house, and all my people shall be ruled according to your word; only in regard to the throne will I be greater than you." And Pharaoh said to Joseph, "See, I have set you over all the land of Egypt." Then Pharaoh took his signet ring off his hand and put it on Joseph's hand; and he clothed him in garments of fine linen and put a gold chain around his neck. (Gen 41.40–42)

By a ring Daniel was glorified in the land of Babylon

During the time of Daniel there ruled a king by the name of Darius, who was so impressed by Daniel that he considered giving his kingdom over to him. However, out of jealousy the other governors and satraps of the king cunningly tricked and persuaded Darius to authorize a decree "that whoever petitions any god or man for thirty days, except [the king], shall be cast into the den of lions" (Dan 6.6). The way this decree was signed was such that it could never be changed,[24] so when the king realized that Daniel would only worship the one true God, he was forced to grudgingly cast him into the den of lions. The brokenhearted king reassured Daniel by saying, "Your God, whom you serve continually, He will deliver you" (Dan 6.16). After this, the king did something very interesting, he sealed the den with a large stone and then sealed the stone with his signet ring and the signet rings of his lords. He did this so that this decision could not be changed. "Then a stone was brought and laid on the mouth of the den, and the king sealed it with his own signet ring and with the signets of his lords, that the purpose concerning Daniel might not be changed" (Dan 6.17). The morning after casting Daniel into the den of lions, the king cried out to Daniel with lamentations.

---

[24]This "way" was unalterable according to the laws of "Persians and the Medes." See Esth 1.19: "If it please the king, let a royal order go forth from him, and let it be written among the laws of the Persians and the Medes so that it may not be altered."

However, Daniel reassured the king that God had saved him from the lions.

Daniel is glorified through the eternal and unwavering decision of being cast into the den of lions, a decision sealed by the signet ring of the house of King Darius. Without the irrevocable decision authorized and sealed with this ring, the glory of God in Daniel would not have been made known to the people of Babylon at this time or in this way. The seal of the signet ring upon the stone shows Daniel's trust in the fidelity of God, through which he becomes empowered as a witness to the people of Babylon. His fidelity is shown to the people who knew that Daniel only needed to renounce his God for thirty days to avoid this punishment. The miracle of Daniel's safety in the lion's den shows the power God gave him. Recalling the role of King Darius' signet ring as an irrevocable seal for decisions and decrees, the rings received by the couple are associated with the eternal decision to follow God. Fr Meyendorff confirms this: ". . . the king of Babylon, with his ring, sealed the lions' den where Daniel was being thrown, as a pledge of his faithfulness to the suffering prophet, a faithfulness which God endorsed by saving Daniel from the lions [Dan 6.17]."[25]

Esther

In the book of Esther, the connection between receiving a signet ring and a house, or household, is made quite apparent. "And Mordecai came before the king, for Esther had told how he was related to her. So the king took off his signet ring, which he had taken from Haman, and gave it to Mordecai; and Esther appointed Mordecai over the house of Haman" (Esth 8.1). The book of Esther presents the power that is shown forth in the symbol of the ring in a way that beautifully relates to the sacramentality and eternal nature of

[25]Meyendorff, *Marriage*, 32.

marriage. "You yourselves write a decree concerning the Jews, as you please, in the king's name, and seal it with the king's signet ring; for whatever is written in the king's name and sealed with the king's signet ring no one can revoke" (Esth 8.8). The last words of this verse are extraordinarily powerful: "For whatever is written in the king's name and sealed with the king's signet ring no one can revoke" (Esth 8.8). We have come to understand that the ring, as a symbol, represents the offering up of a household that consists of a couple united in Christ. However, just as the ring of a king seals an irrevocable and eternal decree, the rings in marriage indicate that marriage is intended to remain steadfast and eternal, as a sacrament that "no one can revoke."[26]

When a signet ring is used, there is nothing that can stop the decree that it seals. Understanding that all good things are of God and are rightly dedicated to him, the responsibility of the married couple is to oversee their new household while glorifying God. "He shall build a house for my name, and I will establish the throne of his kingdom forever" (2 Sam 7.13). Furthermore, the strength of the household is made sure through its dedication to God: "Your house and your kingdom shall be made sure forever before me; your throne shall be established forever" (2 Sam 7.16). With the ring the husband pledges his life in Christ to his wife and the wife to her husband, acting and living in a way that is approved by God: "With the bridal ring, her husband had sacredly pledged [her] to himself."[27] The couple comes together from two different families, two different upbringings, to create a new house, a new family, a new set of rules:

[26]For an explanation of the eternity of marriage see Augustine of Hippo, *On the Good of Marriage* 6 (NPNF[1] 3:402): "To such a degree is that marriage compact entered upon a matter of a certain sacrament, that it is not made void even by separation itself, since, so long as her husband lives, even by whom she has been left, she commits adultery, in case she be married to another: and he who has left her, is the cause of this evil" (cf. Mt 5.32).

[27]Tertullian, *Apology* 6 (ANF 3:22).

completely unique, yet inspired by their experiences with Christ in the world.

The putting on of these rings not only signifies the new household that is to be established for the glory of God, but also indicates that the couple will be as a signet ring on the hand of God himself. Together as one, the married couple represents a unique signet ring, and as such their relationship is gifted to God; their sealed marriage is engraved by their actions. " 'In that day,' says the LORD of hosts, 'I will take you, Zerubbabel My servant, the son of Shealtiel,' says the LORD, 'and will make you like a signet ring; for I have chosen you,' says the LORD of hosts" (Hag 2.23).

Abraham, Isaac, and Rebecca

> O Lord our God, who didst accompany the servant of the patriarch Abraham into Mesopotamia, when he was sent to espouse a wife for his lord Isaac, and who, by means of the drawing of water, didst reveal to him that he should to betroth Rebecca.

Having advanced greatly in age and having been "blessed . . . in all things" (Gen 24.1), Abraham called for the eldest servant of his house. When the servant arrived, Abraham made him swear by the Lord that he would not provide a wife for his son Isaac from the "daughters of Canaanites, among whom [Abraham] dwelled; but [that the servant should] go to [his] country and to [his] family, and take a wife for [his] son Isaac" (Gen 24.3). After refusing to let Isaac go with the servant, Abraham assured the servant that an angel of the Lord would guide him. The servant, along with a caravan of ten camels, went to Mesopotamia, to the city of Nahor (Gen 24.10). When the faithful servant arrived, he prayed that the Lord of all would reveal whom Isaac was to marry.

O LORD God of my master Abraham, please give me success this day, and show kindness to my master Abraham. Behold, here I stand by the well of water, and the daughters of the men of the city are coming out to draw water. Now let it be that the young woman to whom I say, "Please let down your pitcher that I may drink," and she says, "Drink, and I will also give your camels a drink"—let her be the one You have appointed for Your servant Isaac. And by this I will know that You have shown kindness to my master. (Gen 24.12–14)

Before the servant had finished speaking this prayer, Rebecca came with a pitcher on her shoulder and fulfilled this supplication. When this had happened, the servant gave her a gold nose ring and two gold bracelets, and then asked if there was room for him to lodge in her father's house. Upon confirmation of this, the servant gave thanks to the Lord. Rebecca returned to the house to tell her family of what had transpired. Rebecca accepted the proposal and celebrated with her family and the servant. When they returned, the "servant told Isaac all the things that he had done. . . . Then Isaac brought her into his mother Sarah's tent; and he took Rebekah and she became his wife, and he loved her" (Gen 24.66–67).

The story of Isaac and Rebecca is appropriately remembered in the blessing of the rings as an expression of the relationship between God and man. The rings are an expression of God's fidelity, his empowerment, and our relationship with God. The faith of Abraham had grown so much that he confidently sent his servant to find a wife for his son, knowing that God would direct his servant. "He will send His angel before you, and you shall take a wife for my son from there" (Gen 24.7). It was without hesitation that this servant obeyed Abraham, and it was with an open heart that this servant prayed to God. In his prayer he completely relied on God to show him who Isaac was to marry, and when God did so, the servant gave thanks and acknowledged the faithfulness of Abraham. "Then the man bowed down his head and worshiped the LORD. And he said, 'Blessed be the LORD God of my master Abraham, who has not forsaken His mercy and His truth toward my master. As for me, being on the way, the LORD led me to the house of my master's brethren'" (Gen 24.26–27).

When we trust in God, his presence becomes more obvious to us. This trust in the Lord, as shown by Abraham and his servant, must be remembered in marriage and throughout our lives. The same God who guided Rebecca to Isaac through the faith of his people will bond us to one another in marriage. When we acknowledge God in our relationships, we allow ourselves to be perfected in him.

By a ring the uprightness of Tamar was revealed

We find the significance of naming Tamar in this prayer in Genesis 38. In this account, Judah weds his eldest son, Er, to Tamar. However, soon after, Er was killed by the Lord. "But Er, Judah's firstborn, was wicked in the sight of the LORD, and the LORD killed him" (Gen 38.8). After this, Judah sent his second-born, Onan, to marry and have children with Tamar, as was the custom when an elder brother died without leaving heirs. However, Onan did not want to give an heir to his brother, and for his immoral behavior[28] he too was killed by the Lord.[29] After losing two of his sons, Judah felt it wise to not follow the custom, and he prohibited Tamar from marrying his third son, Shelah. Judah instead asked that she "remain a widow in [her] father's house till [his] son Shelah [was] grown" (Gen 38.11). Tamar stayed in her father's house, and while she was

---

[28]See Gen 38.9: "But Onan knew that the heir would not be his; and it came to pass, when he went in to his brother's wife, that he emitted on the ground, lest he should give an heir to his brother."

[29]See Gen 38.10: "And the thing which he did displeased the LORD; therefore He killed him also."

---

there Judah's wife, Shua, died. After being comforted, Judah "went up to his sheepshearers at Timnah" (Gen 38.12). Having heard that Judah had gone to travel and knowing that his third son, Shelah, was grown but had not been given to her, Tamar disguised herself as a prostitute by taking off her widow's garments and covering her face. After doing this, she waited for Judah "in an open place which was on the way to Timnah" (Gen 38.14). Judah saw Tamar, and not recognizing who she was, offered a goat in order to have relations with her. Tamar, being clever, asked for Judah's "signet and cord, and [his] staff that [was in his] hand," as a *pledge*[30] to be given to her until he could give her this goat (Gen 38.18). He willingly agreed, and she conceived by him. After this she left and dressed once again in her garments of widowhood.

Judah sent out a young goat to be given to the prostitute so that his signet ring would be returned, but no one could find her. Three months after Tamar had conceived, Judah was told, "Tamar your daughter-in-law has played the harlot; furthermore she is with child by harlotry" (Gen 38.24). Not knowing that she was pregnant with his child, Judah became enraged and disgusted, and ordered for her to be burned (Gen 38.24). When Tamar was brought to Judah, she said, "By the man to whom these belong, I am with child" (Gen 38.25). She then presented the items given to her and said, "Please determine whose these are—the signet and cord, and staff" (Gen 38.25). Witnessing that this ring and staff belonged to him, Judah replied, "She has been more righteous than I, because I did not give her to Shelah my son" (Gen 38.25).

With the presentation of the signet ring, Judah not only came to understand that he was the father-in-law of this woman whom he was going to kill and the father of the child in her womb, but also that he was more at fault than the person he wanted to put to

---

[30]In this instance, "pledge" is understood to be a type of collateral.

death. The truth of this statement of righteousness is confirmed by the unique signet ring of Judah's house, without which Tamar would have died. Upon the presentation of this ring, Judah became more aware of the sins that he had committed and found himself to be a hypocrite in his own house. He was quick to judge his daughter-in-law of a sin that he also participated in. Furthermore, this sin was committed only because Judah broke his promise to Tamar.

In an unconventional way, Tamar officially entered into the house of Judah, which was promised in her first marriage. With the presentation of the ring and the union to a common house, clarity was brought to the members of the household. Because of this, Judah never had intercourse with Tamar again, nor does Scripture mention him ever getting married after.

The Prodigal Son

In the New Testament we find a presentation of a ring that contrasts with those of the Old Testament. Whereas those who received rings in the Old Testament were deserving and/or entitled to the ring by law, the prodigal son was not. Here, an undeserving son returns home, and a ring is presented as a gift to show welcome, mercy, and grace. This ring shows that there are no bounds to God's gifts of love.

There was a man who had two sons, and the younger of the two asked for his inheritance early. Although most would take offense at being asked for an inheritance early, the father in Christ's story did not hesitate and "divided to them his livelihood" (Lk 15.12). The younger son received his share and went off to a far country, squandering all that he had been given on things the father disapproved of. Having run out of money, the son experienced even more hardship when a famine struck his new land. In desperation he "joined himself to a citizen of that county" (Lk 15.12), working for a pig farmer and feeding his swine. "And he would gladly have filled his stomach with pods that the swine ate, and no one gave him anything" (Lk 15.16). When the son "came to himself" (that is to say, realized the situation he was in), he remembered all the food and servants that he had back in his father's house. "How many of my father's hired servants have bread enough and to spare, and I perish with hunger!" (Lk 15.17). Having come to this realization, the son decided to return to his father's house in the hope that his father would take him back as a hired servant.

As the son was traveling back to his father's house, he started to approach the land from whence he came, and far off in the distance the father of the house "saw him and had compassion, and ran and fell on his neck and kissed him. And the son said to him, 'Father, I have sinned against heaven and in your sight, and am no longer worthy to be called your son'" (Lk 15.20). The father replied by ordering his servants to clothe his son in a robe, put a ring on his right hand, put sandals on his feet, and kill the fatted calf. He ordered his house to celebrate, because his "son was dead and is alive again; he was lost and is found" (Lk 15.24).

In this parable, the prodigal son squandered his inheritance on sin. Yet when he returned, the Father showed mercy and joy. Ringless he abandoned his house, yet at his return he is given a ring signifying that he is reestablished within the family. The Father gives him a ring, which carries the Old Testament symbolism of authority and stewardship. The Father is joyful and gives the symbol of legitimacy. The fidelity of God is shown in the giving of the ring, because it is a sign of mercy and grace, which are ever-flowing from the Trinity. Hoping and dreaming to be a servant, the son is restored as a master in the house that he betrayed. In marriage we must always remember that God restores anything we break and allows us to have new beginnings through the sacraments. Christian couples in

Christ have the right and ability, if not duty, to forgive. Remember that repentance is a sign of God's work in the marriage, and we must always return home to each other as did the prodigal. Just as God forgives and offers new beginnings, so should each of us, most especially between husbands and wives. The classic takeaway line from the 1970 hit movie *Love Story* was "love means never having to say you're sorry." The opposite is true: love means always saying sorry.

Crowns

Another rich and ancient symbol used in marriage is that of crowns. Crowns symbolize the couple's reward for witnessing to Christ and for their faithfulness to him in various ways: as chaste witnesses until the day of marriage, as royalty or stewards over the space and time the couple will share as family, and as prophetic witnesses or martyrs to the truths revealed by Christ. The act of crowning is arguably the oldest symbol of the marriage service. Brides wore crowns with jewels in the late third century,[31] and there is evidence of marriage crowns in the mid- to late fourth century.[32] The ceremonial crowns

[31] If this was not a common custom through the East, it at least may have been in or around Greece. In his exegetical work concerning Revelation 12, St Methodius of Olympus argues that the woman described in the first two verses is a virgin prepared for marriage. What is profitable for us in this explanation is that her appearance includes a crown of stars, which, for St Methodius, appropriately corresponds to jewels upon the bride's head. "Continuing therefore, I beg you to consider this great Woman as representing virgins prepared for marriage. . . . For her robe, she is clothed in pure light; instead of jewels, her head is adorned with shining stars. . . . And she uses the stars as we do gold and brilliant gems." Methodius, *The Symposium: A Treatise on Chastity*, trans. Herbert Musurillo, Ancient Christian Writers 27 (New York: Paulist Press, 1958), 111.

[32] Evidence of marriage crowns being used during this time period is especially evident in the writings of St Gregory of Nazianzus (329–89). Within his oration on holy baptism, he correlates the image of the Church and the bride in marriage. See Gregory Nazianzen, *Orations* 40.18 (NPNF[2] 7:365). "Are you living in Virginity? Be sealed by this purification; make this the sharer and companion of your life. Let this direct your life, your words, every member, every movement, every sense. Honour it,

were not limited to the marriage service, but were most likely also used in some way during baptism.[33] Wedding crowns were usually made of garlands during this time, a trend that would both be preserved and develop into the variety of styles commonly seen today. This imagery is a prevalent and captivating theme within the life of the Church and is found in countless writings, works of art, and hymns. The promise of crowns is expressed in the words and lives of the saints that have gone before us, and is always understood within the context of salvation. Marriage unites the couple to be partner stewards over their family, a little church united in their dedication to Christ. They are crowned to be witnesses and examples of holiness. They die to the fallen world, and in their marriage they are reestablished in their baptismal commitment. This cooperation comes as a response to a gift of love from God.

> O holy God, who didst form man from the dust, and didst fashion woman from his rib, and didst join her unto him as a helper, for it seemed good to Thy majesty that man should not be alone upon the earth: Do Thou, the same Lord, stretch out now also Thy hand from Thy holy dwelling-place, and unite this Thy servant, [*name*], and this Thy handmaiden, [*name*]; for by Thee is the husband joined unto the wife. Unite them in one mind; wed them into one flesh, granting to them the fruit of the body and the procreation of fair children. For Thine is the majesty, and Thine is the kingdom and the power and the glory: of the Father,

that it may honour you; that it may give to your head a crown of graces, and with a crown of delights may shield you."

[33]See Cyril of Jerusalem, *Catechetical Lectures* 3.2 (*NPNF²* 7:14). " 'Let my soul rejoice in the Lord: for He hath clothed me with a garment of salvation, and a robe of gladness: He hath crowned me with a garland as a bridegroom, and decked me with ornaments as a bride' [Is 61.10]: that the soul of every one of you may be found 'not having spot or wrinkle or any such thing' [Eph 5.27]."

and of the Son, and of the Holy Spirit, now and ever and unto ages of ages.

The mystery of two becoming one in the marriage service is repeated many ways to emphasize its importance and centrality to marriage. Crowns are used to show this unity as they are entwined over the couple. There seem to be three prevalent meanings of the crowns that are expressed within the marriage service:

1. The crown as symbol of championship and victory in chastity

2. The crown as symbol of royalty

3. The crown as symbol of martyrdom[34]

The Crown as Symbol of Championship and Victory in Chastity

The action of crowning within the marriage service has its origin in ancient Greece, long before the rise of Christianity. The ancient Olympic games were held there, where the champion was not awarded a gold medal, but rather was crowned with the *kotinos* (κότινος), or crown. This trophy would be made from the wild olive leaves and branches of a sacred olive tree near the temple of Zeus in Olympia. The crowns were simple, yet were representations of power, and were known to be one of the greatest honors a Greek could receive. It was for this honor, this title, this trophy that the Olympians fought and competed.[35] Obtaining such an honor was

---

[34]Fr Alexander Schmemann understood that these were the three representations of crowns in the wedding service, and expressed the importance of this representation as a practical reflection of married life. For further explanation see Schmemann, *Life of the World*, 89–91.

[35]See Herodotus, *The Persian Wars* 8.26 (Godley, LCL). After the Battle of Thermopylae, Xerxes was puzzled as to why so few Greeks were defending the city. Upon learning that they were gathered for the Olympic games, Xerxes inquired once again, "What is the prize for the winner?" He was given the answer, "An olive branch."

obviously a joyous occasion, and this symbol of joy in the olive branch is still present in the Church today in the form of crowns. Fr Schmemann explores the significance of the olive branch: "[I]t was an olive branch which a dove brought to Noah to announce God's forgiveness and reconciliation with man after the Flood. This 'natural' symbolism of oil determined from the beginning its use in the liturgical life of the Church."[36]

As the couple overcomes obstacles, remains chaste, and gains victory over the passions, crowns are awarded to them for their continence. Originally simply garlands, the crowns of marriage were distinct and made for liturgical use, representing honor.[37] The wedding crowns symbolize a reward for purity in life thus far, while it is also upheld as a most honorable future reward—the kingdom of God—for a life of Christian witness to come. This is not to say that the couple will not remain "chaste" after marriage. It is expected that the couple will express their chastity by preserving their bed pure and being intimate only with each other. Here we are simply acknowledging the victory over sin that bride and groom, as husband and wife, are called to. Like the champion Olympians of old, the couple is presented to their spectators and teammates, the laity, as fellow victors.

O Lord our God, Who blessest the crown of the year, and permittest these crowns to be laid on them that are joined to one another by the law of marriage, and thus granting these unto them as the

One of his generals, Tigranes, said, "Good heavens! Mardonius, what kind of men are these against whom you have brought us to fight? Men who do not complete for possessions, but for honor."

[36]Schmemann, *Water and the Spirit*, 51.

[37]See Kenneth Stevenson, *Nuptial Blessing: A Study of Christian Marriage Rites* (New York: Oxford University Press, 1983), 24. In reference to St John Chrysostom the author says, "He seems to imply that the crowns used at weddings are not just any crowns, but special ones, reserved for liturgical use."

reward of chastity, for they are pure that are joined together in the lawfully appointed marriage that is from Thee.[38]

Within the tradition of the Church, crowns have consistently been linked with virginity and purity. It is literally with eternal, heavenly crowns that the virgin saints are rewarded for their steadfastness in the faith, and it is with eternal crowns that the holy martyrs (who will be discussed later in this chapter) are also rewarded. Many hymns of the Church that are attributed to such saints continue to link their holy struggles and that of the Olympians through the theme of "contest." The *apolitikion* of the martyrs expresses this beautifully: "Thy Martyrs, O Lord, in their courageous contest for Thee received as the prize the crowns of incorruption and life from Thee, our immortal God. For since they possessed Thy strength, they cast down the tyrants and wholly destroyed the demons' strengthless presumption." St John Chrysostom viewed the marriage crowns as a sign of purity and continence, which may indicate that crowns were recognized as such in the East as early as the fourth century: "Garlands are wont to be worn on the heads of bridegrooms, as a symbol of victory, betokening that they approach the marriage bed unconquered by pleasure. But if captivated by pleasure he has given himself up to harlots, why does he wear the garland, since he has been subdued?"[39]

At the end of the saint's life on this earth, the contest is ended, the crown is received, and unlike the champions of this world their crowns never fade. "And when the Chief Shepherd appears, you will receive the crown of glory that does not fade away" (1 Pet 5.4). This purity and chastity is remembered in eternity, expressing this reality

[38]*Prayer at the Taking off of the Crowns on the Eighth Day,* in *The Great Book of Needs: Expanded and Supplemented,* vol. 1, *The Holy Mysteries* (South Canaan, PA: St. Tikhon's Seminary Press, 2000), 180.

[39]John Chrysostom, *Homilies on 1 Timothy 9* (NPNF¹ 13:437).

in and outside of time. So, this experience is real, the faithfulness to Christ that is exhibited by the couple is sealed with crowns of honor, and the purity that is expressed in this action is maintained, yet transfigured, in marriage.

The Crown as Symbol of Royalty

> This is what the marriage crowns express: that here is the beginning of a small kingdom which *can* be something like the true Kingdom. The chance will be lost, perhaps even in one night; but at this moment it is still an open possibility. Yet even when it has been lost, and lost again a thousand times, still if two people stay together, they are in a real sense king and queen to each other. And after forty odd years, Adam can still turn and see Eve standing beside him, in a unity with himself which in some small way at least proclaims the love of God's Kingdom.[40]

Mother Alexandra, the founder of Holy Transfiguration women's monastery in Ellwood City, Pennsylvania, often explained that the role of royalty is to take care of the land and all that is attached to it. This is a perfect example of Christian life. As stewards, we care for God's gift, which is given to us both to use it and to care for it.[41] As Adam and Eve are given dominion to care for the earth, the newly married couple is blessed and sent to rule over the place and time that God has given them, that is, the family. In Christ, this time and space is reclaimed to be holy. This little church (your family) will be where God is worshiped and children are taught to respect him. As the crowns are placed on the heads of the couple, the priest prays the following: "O Lord our God, crown them with glory and

---

[40]Schmemann, *Life of the World*, 89–90.
[41]Mother Alexandra offered this explanation in lectures and in conversation with the author (Bp John). [Mother Alexandra was herself a royal: in the world she was known as Princess Ileana of Romania.—*Ed.*]

honor." It is not merely with words and a contract that the couple is crowned, but it is with glory and honor from God that the couple is blessed to become a new family, a little church, in which they are king and queen.

The state of being crowned is one of order, and this "ordering" is an ordination, which God has prepared for those who are called to marriage. In the world, a king is crowned to receive the responsibility of being the head of state. His royalty is his position of authority, and he will forever live within this order or position. Sacramentally, being crowned in the state of marriage expresses one's position of responsibility to one another, and, if granted children, responsibility to them as well. The family, for both the crowned queen and king of this marriage, becomes a country sustained in its service to the God who established it.

All power and authority for Christians is expressed through service. Our Lord showed us the importance of serving one another by girding himself and washing the feet of his servants. He loves first, and then further shows his leadership by serving and caring for those who are gathered around him. So ought Christian husbands and wives love and care for each other, and lead their children by serving them. It is the sacred responsibility of the parents to impart to their children a sense of their Christian responsibilities. This means guiding them to become fruitful citizens of the society they live in as well as of the kingdom of heaven. They need to be cared for with love, respect, and service. Christ treated his disciples as friends, not as servants. The late Dr John Boojamra, Christian Education Department Chair for the Antiochian Archdiocese, taught that it is the responsibility of parents to care for their children with the same respect and attention that is given to guests in their home. It is not the job of the children to take out the trash, because the trash belongs to the owners of the home. Children will grow to have their own homes and their own trash. Rather, it is the job of parents to equip their children to be good citizens.

The Crown as Symbol of Martyrdom

"No shuddering fear of spirits lurks within, for the plague has been driven away in flight from thy people, and Christ dwells in all thy streets, Christ is everywhere. It is as if this home-land of martyrs had been destined for the sacred crowns, there rises from it towards heaven such a company of its high-born citizens clad in snow-white robes."[42] With these words the Roman poet Aurelius Prudentius Clemens expressed through the symbol of crowns the honor granted to the martyrs by God. While oppressed by those who wore earthly crowns and who obeyed the laws of men, the martyrs pursued the Truth and gave up their lives for Christ. Marriage, too, calls for us to lay down our lives for Christ, not necessarily by dying, but by sacrificing our own desires and wants for the wellbeing of the other, even unto death. In this self-sacrificial dedication to the other, the spouses communally experience the joy of Christ through service. St John Chrysostom shares his thoughts in this way:

> For He espoused her as a wife, He loves her as a daughter, He provides for her as a handmaid, He guards her as a virgin, He fences her round like a garden, and cherishes her like a member: as a head He provides for her, as a root He causes her to grow, as a shepherd He feeds her, as a bridegroom He weds her, as a propitiation He pardons her, as a sheep He is sacrificed, as a bridegroom He preserves her in beauty, as a husband He provides for her support.[43]

[42]Prudentius, *Crowns of Martyrdom* 4.69–76 (Thomson, LCL).
[43]John Chrysostom, *Two Homilies on Eutropius* 2.15 (NPNF[1] 9:262–63).

Before the final blessing of the marriage, the priest prays that God will "take up their crowns."[44] This image is an encouragement for married couples to live in holiness and follow the ways of the martyrs and married saints to salvation. Salvation is a gift that is tried by many obstacles and temptations; yet, it is expressed as joyful life in the presence of God in his kingdom. This joy is not as fleeting or simple as temporary "happiness." Rather, it contains within itself the fruits of labor and assists in the development of the unquenchable desire to serve the other in accordance with one's natural inclination as a communal being.

Then secondly, the glory and the honor is that of the martyr's crown. For the way to the Kingdom is the *martyria*—bearing witness to Christ. And this means crucifixion and suffering. A marriage which does not constantly crucify its own selfishness and self-sufficiency, which does not "die to itself" that it may point beyond itself, is not a Christian marriage. The real sin of marriage today is not adultery or lack of "adjustment" or "mental cruelty." It is the idolization of the family itself, the refusal to understand marriage as directed toward the Kingdom of God.[45]

Crowns become the reward for and sign of carrying the cross. Before marriage a specific cross is given to the individual, but now a new cross is given to the two united as one. This new cross requires cohesive work with the other in a way that is unique to the individual and is bearable only in service to Christ, through the spouse, by the Holy Spirit, and in concordance with the Father. In this sacrificial love, martyrdom is made manifest. Again, in the words of Fr Schmemann:

---

[44]Found in the prayer for crowns in the wedding service.
[45]Schmemann, *Life of the World*, 90. Italics in original.

In a Christian marriage, in fact, three are married; and the united loyalty of the two toward the third, who is God, keeps the two in an active unity with each other as well as with God. Yet it is the presence of God which is the death of the marriage as something only "natural." It is the cross of Christ that brings the self-sufficiency of nature to its end. But "by the cross joy [and not 'happiness!'] entered the whole world." Its presence is thus the real joy of marriage. It is the joyful certitude that the marriage vow, in the perspective of the eternal Kingdom, is not taken "until death parts," but until death unites us completely.[46]

The Common Cup

There is something about eating and drinking that joins us together. Sharing meals involves preparation, participation, and reception. This experience is universal among all cultures and is how families share life together. In sharing food, they share time, conversation, dreams, and pains. Sharing meals is for more than physical nourishment; rather, gathering around the table and eating together generates oneness. The experience of eating and drinking has always been an intimate act. The Eucharist (the body and blood of Christ: "communion") is offered to the communicants as food that unites us to God and to each other. This sacrament allows us to be fed by God in heaven in a way that mortal man can relate to: through food and drink.

Due to the scarcity of clean water in the Middle East during the time of Jesus, wine was more of a necessity than the luxury we may think of it as today.[47] Being a plant, grape vines allow for a unique process to take place, in which water is taken in by the plant and

---

[46]Schmemann, *Life of the World*, 90–91. Bracketed comment in original.
[47]Leland Ryken, James C. Wilhoit, and Tremper Longman III, eds., *Dictionary of Biblical Imagery* (Downers Grove, IL: IVP Academic, 1998), s.v. "wine."

filtered, producing fruit containing clean water that is safe to eat. The grapes were processed to make juice or wine, and for this reason wine, as a necessity, easily became a symbol for sustenance and life.[48] The alcohol produced by the microorganisms used in winemaking killed dangerous germs, allowing the wine to be life-preserving and to thus become the staple drink of the time. Representing both blood or "life-fluid,"[49] wine, at the time of Jesus and even to this day, has been and is still used in Jewish rites and ceremonies.[50] For instance, it is still customary for Orthodox Jews to add a small portion of wine to a small jar of water in remembrance of "the Ten Plagues of Egypt: the mixture, called 'blood,' is cast on the ground before the house."[51] Furthermore, the Jewish marriage rite elaborates this connection between life and wine, and without the partaking of wine in the rite, it would be impossible for the betrothal or marriage to "take place."[52] Understanding this connection between life and wine, it becomes obvious that at the Last Supper Christ was emphasizing that he was giving his disciples life itself in the partaking of his body and blood. So here, too, sharing in "life" from a common cup confirms the presence and action of Jesus Christ.

Wine as a symbol of joy, truth, atonement, and union with God is made clear and confirmed by the Gospel reading about the wedding in Cana of Galilee where Jesus turned water into wine. Water jars containing about twenty to thirty gallons in total for ritual washings are spoken of in the Gospel reading. Jesus changed this water

[48]Ibid.

[49]Here, "life-fluid" is "representative of powers which bestow, nourish, increase, preserve, and reproduce life." E. S. Drower, *Water Into Wine: A Study of Ritual Idiom in the Middle East* (London: Murray, 1956), 7.

[50]Ibid., 61. "It [wine] plays, of course, an integral part in the Jewish domestic rites, and its character as a 'life-fluid,' that is to say, a symbol of life fecund and reproductive, is evident in many Oriental Jewish ceremonies and customs."

[51]Ibid., 63.

[52]Ibid., 61. "No Jewish betrothal or marriage can take place without ceremonial wine."

that was set aside for ritual washing, and not for drinking. This miracle shows his authority as God to bless and give life. He took that which is of this world and used it for the kingdom of God. He took water for cleansing and made it new life, the Life that he himself is, and which, once given, will well up within us. He takes water for cleansing and cleanses us of sin and restores us to communion with himself. In being present at this feast and transforming water into wine, Christ confirms the state of marriage as something that is honorable, blessed, and transformative. Therefore, the blessed wine of the common cup is a sign that a transformation is taking place. Likewise, when we allow Christ to work in our marriage, he will change our earthly efforts into gifts from heaven.

Notwithstanding the connection with eating and drinking, and the ritual heritage passed down from the Jews, the liturgical use of the common cup finds its origin in something much deeper—in the life of the Church, the holy Eucharist. It is undeniable that marriage took place in the context of the eucharistic celebration up until the tenth century, and included the reception of the Eucharist until the fifteenth century.[53] In fact, the earliest process by which marriage was conducted included a civil marriage followed by the couple's participation in the liturgy, and concluded with the blessing of the bishop.[54] However, the wine of the common cup has, over time, replaced the Eucharist in the wedding service in response to the emergence of marriages involving people from churches in schism. Although the Eucharist is absent from the marriage service as a separate rite, the sacramentality of the marriage itself cannot be denied. The Church maintains that every sacrament is fulfilled and finds meaning in the Eucharist. The common cup points to the Eucharist as the essential

---

[53]This is true at least in the Slavic tradition; in the Greek tradition the Eucharist may have been more commonly absent from the marriage service in the thirteenth century. See Meyendorff, *Marriage*, 28.

[54]Ibid., 21, 24–25.

food for heavenly life from Christ and reminds the couple of this. In the wedding at Cana, Christ took the water for ritual cleansing and made it the finest wine. He took that which is of this world and used it to point to and reveal that which is beyond this world. He took that which is necessary for life and made it life-giving: his own blood and life. According to Fr Meyendorff,

> What makes a "sacrament" is not necessarily a set of specific, visible gestures, accomplished by a valid minister. Actually, the Church itself—a mysterious union of God with His people—is the Sacrament, the Mystery of salvation. . . . When man is incorporated into this union through Baptism, this is indeed "sacrament," for the Mystery of salvation is applied to the individual commitment of that man. But all these individual "sacraments" are "completed" in the Eucharist.[55]

For Orthodox Christians, "sacrament" means God's action in our lives. Marriage is undoubtedly a sacrament because it is God who extends his arm and makes us husband and wife, because it is for salvation, and because the consequence of the marriage is an eternal relationship. Just as your parents will always be your parents and your children will always be your children, your spouse, whom you married on a particular date in your history, will always be your spouse.

The Gospel Book, the Great Censing, and the Dance of Isaiah

The Church gives us the opportunity to grow and experience true life in Christ. She does this by providing liturgical services and programs that serve the world. Both are means by which the Church teaches us to grow closer to God. Like children learning to live in the world, we learn to grow by the instruction and life of the Church.

[55]Ibid., 22.

We are taught how to partake of the Eucharist, the divine banquet, just as children are taught to eat at the dinner table. We are taught to pray together so that we may commune with God, like children who are learning to speak. And, like children taking their first steps, we process first to the Gospel Book on the table, and later dance around the Gospel Book, taking our first steps as a married couple.

When a child takes his or her first steps, we know something wonderful is happening. The parents get excited at seeing their children grow, and all in the room encourage the child to continue. Even though everyone in the room knows that these steps may mean more work for the parents, more potential danger for the child, and a greater need for watchfulness, everyone is encouraging and excited because of all the wonderful things that come with growing. The Church also teaches husband and wife how to take these first steps in their new life united to each other. The first steps of the couple are not taken in a rush, nor are they painstakingly taken. Rather, the first steps of the couple are taken in a liturgical procession followed by a liturgical dance. Encouraging us in our dance are the prophets, martyrs, and apostles.

At the conclusion of the betrothal service, we are now introduced to the marriage rite itself. This transition, which in some traditions is a physical movement farther into the church after the betrothal is celebrated in the vestibule or middle of the church nave, is done with the singing of verses from Psalm 128, which describe the fruits of marriage. This is done in the Antiochian tradition by the bishop, if he is present, or by the priest, if the bishop is not present during the great censing.

> Blessed is every one who fears the Lord, who walks in his ways!
> You shall eat the fruit of the labor of your hands; you shall be
>   happy, and it shall be well with you.
> Your wife will be like a fruitful vine within your house;

Your children will be like olive shoots around your table.

Lo, thus shall the man be blessed who fears the Lord.

The Lord bless you from Zion!

May you see the prosperity of Jerusalem all the days of your life!

May you see your children's children!

Peace be upon Israel!

These verses, which are followed by the refrain "Glory to Thee, our God, Glory to Thee," were chanted in ancient days while the Levites were entering the temple for the great feast of Atonement in Israel.[56] It would have been these words that were sung as the high priest censed the ark of the covenant. We now sing these same verses as the priest or bishop censes the Gospel Book, the church, the couple, and the people.[57] The priest censes around the table and Gospel Book, which would have corresponded in ancient times to the tablets Moses received from God, on which were written the Ten Commandments.

The marriage service is transformative and unites us to each other and to Christ. In the marriage service, the dance of Isaiah takes place as a journey around the table and Gospel Book. The dance of Isaiah is a joyful procession, a journey in which the Church is blessing the "going out and coming in"[58] of the couple. This dance joins the visible with the invisible, the Church on earth with the kingdom of heaven. The Old Testament word of God is fulfilled in Christ the eternal Word, as represented here by the Gospel Book. The priest processes with the couple in a circular motion, which indicates the eternity of marriage. It is noteworthy that this procession occurs in three of our sacraments—baptism, ordination, and marriage—and

---

[56]See Michel Najim, *The Theology of the Orthodox Sacrament of Matrimony and its Implication in our Family Life*, 8.

[57]In some traditions the censing has been eliminated from the service. Fr Schmemann said that it was omitted because people associated incense with funerals.

[58]This is found in the prayer said immediately after the removal of the crowns.

that these same verses sung in the marriage service are also sung at ordinations, although in a different order. In all three of these services, there is a dedication of the person to God in a new capacity. In baptism this new capacity is as a Christian; in marriage this new capacity is as a united couple in God; and in ordination it is as a deacon, priest, or bishop. These verses reflect on the joy of the incarnation of Christ and the joy experienced in light of the martyrdom that we are called to in our new capacity as husband and wife. As the couple processes around the Gospel Book while being led by the priest, the following verses are chanted:

> Rejoice, O Isaiah! A virgin is with child; and shall bear a Son, Emmanuel: He is both God and man; and Orient is His name; magnifying Him, we call the virgin blessed.

> O holy martyrs, who fought the good fight and have received your crowns: Entreat ye the Lord, that He will have mercy on our souls.

> Glory to Thee, O Christ God, the apostles' boast, the martyrs' joy, whose preaching was the consubstantial Trinity.

In every instance of every service, the Gospel Book represents Jesus Christ, the Word of God, who is the ultimate example for us. Throughout the betrothal and wedding service, the Gospel Book is rested upon the wedding table so that the bride and groom facing it understand that they are dedicating themselves to Christ in every moment of their marriage. The Gospel Book contains all the readings for each Sunday and major feast day that the Church has felt necessary for us to hear throughout the year. With this in mind, the couple journeys around the table with these life-giving lessons and teachings of Christ at the center.

PART III

Walking through the Marriage Ceremony

Within Orthodoxy the theology of marriage is the same, but marriage ceremony customs can be quite different from jurisdiction to jurisdiction. There are even variations between ancient churches and from village to village. These differences are helpful for understanding both how the Church adapts to local cultures and how flexible the Church really is. We will note some of these differences to give us a deeper and more colorful understanding of this mystery of marriage.

The marriage ceremony is in no way the start of the process of marriage. The ceremony is the culmination of a couple's choice (sometimes with more or less influence from parents, family, or even clergy) and the almost ritualistic gatherings of the families. Families come together, often on their best behavior (though some are not), to negotiate and navigate the process. In some Middle Eastern villages, after several days of gatherings, the groom's family goes to the bride's home on the wedding day to accompany the bride and her clan to the church, where the bride meets the groom and the priest, who leads the couple followed by the guests to the altar to begin the services. In some traditions the betrothal service is celebrated in the vestibule of the church. Often in America, and now with satellite movies and programming entering the homes of the Middle East, the bride is ushered by her father to the altar and presented to the groom for marriage. It is interesting to note that in an age of equality, many brides still want to be given away by their fathers instead of claiming ownership of themselves.

Throughout history, people have married for the sake of social status, tax breaks, and to beget children that could help on the farm or with the family business. With these reasons mostly gone, many people now marry to forge a partnership that can, or should, bring them salvation, and to live a Christian way of life. Today, it is generally agreed that we should avoid any kind of forced marriage. In modern times, coercion at the time of marriage often leads to resentment and makes the already difficult process of growing through the challenges of uniting to one another even more difficult. In the Slavic and Antiochian traditions, the bride and groom are asked if they have free will to marry. This interrogation is absent from the books of the Greek Church, and is reported to have been first added in Kiev at the time of St Peter Moghila (seventeenth century).[1] The acceptance of these questions reflects the Church's desire for the two to marry of their own free will. There are many poor reasons to marry, such as keeping the money in the family, merging companies, or maintaining peace treaties. Choosing to marry, and choosing to marry a particular person, gives modern people the encouragement to do the hard work of staying married and building an Orthodox marriage. As the adage goes, "Choose your love and love your choice."

Before the ceremony begins, the priest asks the groom and then the bride:

PRIEST: Do you, [name], have a good, free and unconstrained will and a firm intention to take as your wife this woman, [name], whom you see here before you?

---

[1]Meyendorff, *Marriage*, 34–35.

BRIDEGROOM: I have, reverend father.

. . .

PRIEST: Do you, [*name*], have a good, free and unconstrained will and a firm intention to take as your husband this man, [*name*], whom you see here before you?

BRIDE: I have, reverend father.

The Betrothal Service begins with:

PRIEST: Blessed is our God, always, now and ever and unto ages of ages.

CHOIR: Amen.

In this exclamation blessing God, we set ourselves in a correct relationship with God, who alone is eternal, good, and sovereign. When we were growing up, my younger brother regularly reminded me when I got a bit too bossy that "There is but one God, and you are not him." Blessing God puts us in a correct relationship in which we know that the Lord is God, and we are but his. We are his delight, his creation, and even his servants, but surely not his equals. The choir's "amen" shows that the people confirm this exclamation, because "amen" means "so be it" and expresses the approval and ratification of those who say it.

After establishing that the God whom we address is the One who is God and whom we know to be the giver of marriage, a fact that will be emphatically proclaimed in this ceremony, we make petitions that set before God all of our needs, hopes, and desires. Setting these needs forth first allows us to enter into a "prayer space" without earthly concerns. We express this so beautifully in the Divine Liturgy when we sing with the angels, "Let us who mystically represent the cherubim . . . lay aside all earthly cares." The first three petitions each include the word "peace," but each uses the word differently.

PRIEST: In peace let us pray to the Lord.

CHOIR: Lord, have mercy.

This "peace" means being in Christ. It is the image of the Old Testament "*shalom*," which is peace in God. We who are baptized into Christ pray liturgically *in* Christ, the high priest, as we gather as the assembly of the Church. The Church itself is in Christ, and in Christ, we can ask anything of the Father in Christ's name, as Christ promised us (see Jn 14.13). All of Orthodox corporate or liturgical worship is offered up in Christ.

PRIEST: For the peace from above and for the salvation of our souls, let us pray to the Lord.

CHOIR: Lord, have mercy.

This "peace" is God's grace sent to us from above for our salvation. Because it is from above, it is a gift of God, not created by man and not in man's control. In 1 Corinthians 1.3 we read, "Grace [be] unto you, and peace from God our Father, and [from] the Lord Jesus Christ." In James 1.17 we read, "Every good gift and every perfect gift is from above, and cometh down from the Father of Lights." Marriage itself is a gift that we can choose to receive. If (or rather, *when*) the going gets tough and we need to do some work to understand and love each other, it is helpful to know that God has given us each other and marriage as a gift. He has given these to us, so that our success—or rather, his success—comes from our accepting the gift, not changing each other. Understanding comes from having the same Holy Spirit sealed in each of us and in marriage, uniting us to each other. If we can purify our lenses (that is, our perspectives and interpretations) and can have good will, the Holy Spirit will guide us and we will come to share in the Truth. Some imagine that they can mold another person. We can change only ourselves, and the other needs to choose how he or she will respond. Accepting each other as a gift and using God's grace to heal and grow allows us to transform and be changed by God. This is both a miracle and a paradox. It comes from sharing in God's grace and living life together for and in him.

PRIEST: For the peace of the whole world, for the welfare of the holy churches of God, and for the union of all, let us pray to the Lord.

CHOIR: Lord, have mercy.

This "peace" of the world is a peace without war. It is good to call upon Christ, who in John 16.33 explains: "These things I have spoken unto you, that in me you might have peace. In the world you shall have tribulation: but be of good cheer; I have overcome the world." Surely if the world understood and accepted what it means to be in Christ, there would be peace on earth. Many commentators say that the prayer for the welfare of the holy churches of God is a prayer to heal the schisms of the Church. The experience of schism is particularly painful when Christians of separated confessions marry. It is certainly difficult to choose between parishes, choose which church to baptize children in, and choose to go to communion in separate places. In this petition we pray for the union of our separated brethren and ask God to bring union and stability to the churches. This is of course a monumental task beyond the scope of this work. Suffice it to say that in this petition we pray for this union and ask couples who come together from separated churches to work hard at discerning what God wants for them as well as for their future children.

Typically, pastors do not encourage prospective spouses to become Orthodox just for the ceremony, but rather recommend that they study the faith and make an informed decision for themselves. This does not mean that we do not want the spouses of Orthodox to embrace the faith, but rather ask that they embrace the faith out of free will. Nevertheless, we acknowledge that it is difficult when a family's time is split between different churches and the whole family cannot commune together. We pray for the restoration of the unity of the churches because it is good for families to belong to strong, healthy, right-believing and worshiping communities. A strong parish can witness to families better than a divided one. This is true on every level, whether we are considering the sixty thousand divided Christian communities, the multiple overlapping jurisdictions, struggles within a diocese, or strife within a parish.

PRIEST: For this holy house and for those who enter with faith, reverence, and the fear of God, let us pray to the Lord.

CHOIR: Lord, have mercy.

Our petitions, which started out on a more global scale, now begin to focus on a more local level. Here we focus on the parish community. When the parish is strong, it can be a support to the new family, which is to be a "little church" where God is praised, sanctifying the space and time of the home. From the community, family members receive support, positive models of being Christian men and women, and examples of good parenting. Strong parishes support and enrich the families that they serve. The people of the church are people of faith. They are in Christ, and he is their faith and strength. We are people who revere God and stand in awe of him. We do not fear him as one who wants to destroy us; rather, he is one who is awesome.

PRIEST: For His Beatitude, our Metropolitan [*name*], and for His (Eminence, Grace), our (Archbishop, Bishop) [*name*], for the honorable priesthood, the diaconate in Christ, for all the clergy and the people, let us pray to the Lord.

CHOIR: Lord, have mercy.

God gives every church all of the charisms, or gifts, that it needs to serve the people. By "church" here we mean a local bishop surrounded by his presbyters and people. While not every bishop, presbyter, and parish has all of the gifts, every diocese does. The bishop, and by extension the presbyters, is set aside to guard and teach the faith in order to protect the people. A strong bishop with healthy clergy and people will together have all of the resources and talents necessary for the family to know God and raise children in a holy and Orthodox way. The archdiocese and diocese support the parishes, who support the people.

PRIEST: For the servant of God [*name*], and for the handmaiden of God [*name*], who now plight each other their troth, and for their salvation, let us pray to the Lord.

CHOIR: Lord, have mercy.

Our God knows us by name, even from our mother's womb. The Church recognizes the couple by name as they plight (solemnly promise) each other their troth (faith or loyalty). In this petition we pray for the couple as they promise to be faithful, genuine, honest, and real. This fidelity is also accompanied by many dreams and hopes, as well as a common understanding of Christian family life, which leads to salvation. By sacrificing for each other, serving each other, obeying each other, and loving each other, we will grow in love for God and mature in our common faith, which is Jesus Christ.

PRIEST: That they may be granted children for the continuation of the race, and all their petitions which are unto salvation, let us pray to the Lord.

CHOIR: Lord, have mercy.

Procreation is a blessed responsibility of mankind. God created us male and female, allowing us to procreate, which is an image of God's ability to create. Just as when God creates it expresses his love, our procreation expresses the love that God gives us for each other. Furthermore, we ask God to give us all of our petitions that are unto our salvation; thus we recognize that we do not always know what is best for us. Because we trust God, who is good and has shown himself to be trustworthy, we trust God to hear our prayer and give us what is best for us. Trusting God is a learned trait and takes practice and courage. We learn how to trust God by trusting him and seeing how he works good in our lives. Just as a child learns to ride a bike by riding, we learn to trust God by trusting him. This requires persistence and patience.

PRIEST: That He will send down upon them perfect and peaceful love, and assistance, let us pray to the Lord.

CHOIR: Lord, have mercy.

God is love and is the giver of love. The love that we seek comes from God and is perfect, unlike human love, which may be distorted and limited. Perfect and peaceful love is a gift from God and goes beyond human expressions of love, which are often selfish. This love reflects the unity and love of the Trinity and is a gift. This perfect love is a miraculous gift, because only God can give perfect love, and he invites us to experience it. Saying that this love comes "down upon them" indicates that God sends us his love.

Some people complain that marriage is difficult. It is difficult when we do not live for each other and then fear that our needs will not be met. This manifests itself in the fear that others will take advantage of us. If, however, we live for the other and the other responds without fear, God's love will carry us and bring us closer to himself and to each other. Our very relationship with our spouse is with and in Christ, and our love of God brings us closer to him and to each other. Likewise, our love for each other brings us out of ourselves and closer to God. To be thankful for the gift of love, that is, each other, God allows us to know love and be strengthened by it.

We need to learn how to be vulnerable to God and each other. This is difficult as we so value self-reliance. To be self-sufficient ultimately means that we do not need God. However, needing God and each other is essential for salvation because it is simply impossible to save ourselves. Learning to appropriately need each other is good and holy. We are not talking about an unhealthy dependency or co-dependency here, but about that which in modern usage is called a "healthy interdependency" with a partner, and a healthy reliance on and acceptance of God's work in our lives. This acceptance should come without pride or confusion because "every good and perfect gift is from above" (Jas 1.17).

PRIEST: That He will preserve them in oneness of mind, and in steadfast faith, let us pray to the Lord.

CHOIR: Lord, have mercy.

Human understanding is limited by experience and interpretation. Disharmony comes from different perspectives and biases based on past experiences interpreted through goals and ideals. When two people who are partnered together in marriage share and accept the goals and truths that come as gifts from God, and when they put away sinful biases and distortions through the process of forgiveness and healing, they will be blessed by God with oneness of mind and steadfastness of faith. This faith is Christ. This oneness allows us to understand issues and opportunities in our lives the same way and come to the same conclusions.

Married persons who distrust each other or who fear that their needs will not be met in the marriage seem to compete with each other. This competition leads to arguing even when they agree! We might ask why couples fight at all. Fighting has been shown to be an attempt at intimacy. When we fight, we go after each other, penetrating each other's space. When we want intimacy, but do not trust each other enough to be vulnerable with each other, we can fight. This does not mean that we want couples to fight, but rather that we recognize their desire for intimacy and wish for them to find healthier ways to meet these intimate needs.

When couples have difficulty coming to an understanding, we recommend six simple rules:

• Fight with good will, knowing that you are on the same side.

• Fight for the purpose of understanding.

• Repeat back what you are hearing to check for accuracy.

• Stay on the topic, putting aside what happened last year or forty years ago.

• Refrain from name-calling and words like "always" and "never."

• Own your own feelings and thoughts, refraining from telling each other what the other thinks.

PRIEST: That He will preserve them in a blameless way of life, let us pray to the Lord.

CHOIR: Lord, have mercy.

PRIEST: That the Lord our God will grant to them an honorable marriage and a bed undefiled, let us pray to the Lord.

CHOIR: Lord, have mercy.

We are living in a supersized and supersexed world. It takes great self-control and discipline to avoid sin and live in a blameless way. Marriage itself will not take away our "supersized" passions and temptations. Human beings are attracted to novelty and act compulsively. We ultimately seek fulfillment and refreshment that can come only from the "living water" (Jn 7.38) that our Creator is and gives. When marriage relationships include Christ, Christ can strengthen us and deliver us, but such fulfillment requires our acceptance of God's will and our willingness to let God work in us.

PRIEST: For our deliverance from all affliction, wrath, danger, and necessity, let us pray to the Lord.

CHOIR: Lord, have mercy.

Often people ask about writing their own prayers and vows for a wedding service. Sometimes we ask them to make a list of all of the things they would ask in their prayers. As we read the ceremony, we then check off all that is already covered. It is rare that we do not check off everything on the list. In this petition we ask God to protect us from tribulation, which Fr Schmemann says includes civil unrest; wrath, which manifests in hurricanes, floods, earthquakes, foreign invasions, and famine; danger, such as in the form of robbers and thieves, accidents, and harm from human and mechanical errors; and necessity, which is poverty, or a lack of knowledge, understanding, or resources.[2] We ask to be delivered from everything here that would distract us from living godly lives with each other. For this reason, we pray for civil authorities and seasonable weather as well.

PRIEST: Help us, save us, have mercy on us, and keep us, O God, by Thy grace.

CHOIR: Lord, have mercy.

Just in case the wedding guests missed something while we intoned the petitions (perhaps they were remembering how cute the bride was when she was in kindergarten), again we affirm God's real action in our lives, and the importance of his grace for our salvation.

PRIEST: Commemorating our most holy, most pure, most blessed and glorious Lady Theotokos and ever-virgin Mary with all the Saints, let us commend ourselves and each other, and all our life unto Christ our God.

CHOIR: To Thee, O Lord.

---

[2]Schmemann, "Theology of Marriage" (lecture).

By calling to remembrance the Birth-giver of God, and the saints who in every generation worship and love her Son, we can have confidence that the Christ we commend ourselves to is the Christ who was born of a virgin, was crucified for our sins, and rose from the dead. The Christ we commend ourselves to cannot be reduced to an image in our heads or a historic figure that we ourselves mold and interpret based on our books; rather, he is the Word of the living God, who is a person and takes on flesh. He allows us to encounter him in our lives, and most particularly in our primary relationship with our spouse. To understand the word "remember," it helps to look at the word "dismember." To dismember means to take something apart, but to remember something is to put it back together and make it present now. Marriage takes place in the Church, which is the body of Christ. In the body of Christ is also his mother, whom he lifted up from the dead upon her dormition, as well as all those who from the beginning of the world until its end say "yes" to God and share in his life. After calling to remembrance the mother of God and the saints and having dedicated ourselves to Christ, we exclaim why this is reasonable in the following petition:

PRIEST: For unto Thee are due all glory, honor, and worship: to the Father, and to the Son, and to the Holy Spirit, now and ever and unto ages of ages.

CHOIR: Amen.

In saying "amen," the people seal all of these petitions as their own. They have gathered together to pray for the bride and groom, to support them and share this God-given event with them, and to be part of an assembly of the entire Church seen and unseen. When the local parish assembles for the marriage in Christ's name to act as Church, the couple witness to their guests their faith in Christ, who established this Church and is its source. Now that we have expressed many of our concerns, which could otherwise distract us from our prayer, by laying them at the feet of Christ, we are now prepared to offer our first prayer to God.

PRIEST: O eternal God, who hast brought into unity those who were sundered, and hast ordained for them an indissoluble bond of love, who didst bless Isaac and Rebecca, and didst make them heirs of Thy promise: Bless also these Thy servants, [*name*] and [*name*], guiding them unto every good work. For Thou art a good God and lovest mankind, and unto Thee we ascribe glory: to the Father, and to the Son, and to the Holy Spirit, now and ever and unto ages of ages.

CHOIR: Amen.

It is the eternal God who unites a man and a woman in marriage, and who has set up the world in such a way so as to have them share his love. By saying "his love," we mean the love that God the Father shares with God the Son and God the Holy Spirit. This love is the same love that God shared with Abraham as well as his son Isaac and Isaac's wife Rebecca: a love that brings us to a covenant that is essential for salvation history. Abraham prayed for a child and God granted his wish with a son, Isaac, but Abraham needed to show his faithfulness and trust in God and be willing to do anything God asked. Isaac, who was spared from being sacrificed, is twice given by God as a gift rewarding Abraham's faithfulness. It is with Abraham that God makes the covenant to be our God and to make us his people (Gen 17.2–9).[3]

God blesses the bride and groom, dedicating them to good works or godly life as a mercy. This "mercy" is to be their God and give

---

[3]See Part II under the section "Rings" for more on this image (pp. 37–49).

them salvation. Much of what will help them grow will come from all of the hurts and reconciliations as well as sacrifices necessary for every marriage. God will allow this marriage to help two separate persons grow or mature into a united expression of the Holy Trinity. Marriage pains will mold Christian witnesses who will receive crowns of glory, which is salvation.

PRIEST: Peace be unto all.

CHOIR: And to your spirit.

Peace is the paramount gift of God. It is an expression of God himself—his grace, his love, his joining himself to us. When Christ appeared to his disciples after his crucifixion, he blessed them with peace and said to them again, "Peace unto you: as my Father has sent me, even so I send you" (Rom 1.7). This peace of Christ is remembered in every blessing given by a bishop or priest, who forms the Greek initials of Jesus Christ, IC XC, with his hand when he blesses. The reception of this peace is, for the bride and groom, a way of being united with God and each other. God's peace transfigures us and allows us to transcend the earthly; what was earthly is now made heavenly by peace and grace.

PRIEST: Bow your heads unto the Lord.

CHOIR: To Thee, O Lord.

The bowing of the head is an ancient and universal action of subservience and respect to God. We acknowledge our need to be right with God, and that God is not a "buddy," but our Lord. Bowing our head to him allows us to acknowledge and experience this realistic positioning of ourselves in relation to him. If God were reducible to

---

a "buddy," we would be left without a God. "But this command I gave them: 'Obey my voice, and I will be your God, and you shall be my people. And walk in all the way I have commanded you, that it may be well with you'" (Jer 7.23).

PRIEST: O Lord our God, who hast espoused the Church as a pure virgin from among the gentiles: Bless this betrothal, and unite and maintain these Thy servants in peace and oneness of mind. For unto Thee are due all glory, honor, and worship: to the Father, and to the Son, and to the Holy Spirit, now and ever and unto ages of ages.

CHOIR: Amen.

Christ, whom we call the Bridegroom, espouses the Church, calling her out from among the Gentiles. This Christ, who also attended the marriage feast at Cana, is now called upon to bless this marriage service and to grant peace, oneness of mind, and marital unity to the bride and groom. Christ himself is the one who grants marriage and is the priest who gives marital unity. This is in contrast to other views of marriage, which emphasize that the couple contract the marriage themselves by their mutual agreement. For the Orthodox, it is Christ (through his bishop or priest) who blesses marriage and allows the couple to be united in him.

Then taking the rings, the priest blesses the bridal pair, making the sign of the cross with the ring of the bride over the bridegroom, and with that of the bridegroom over the bride, saying to the man:

[PRIEST:] The servant of God, [*name*], is betrothed to the hand-maiden of God, [*name*], in the name of the Father, and of the Son, and of the Holy Spirit. Amen.

And to the woman:

[PRIEST:] The handmaiden of God, [*name*], is betrothed to the servant of God, [*name*], in the name of the Father, and of the Son, and of the Holy Spirit. Amen.

And when he has said this to each of them three times, he places the rings on their right hands. Then the bridal pair exchanges the rings, and the priest says the following prayer:

PRIEST: Let us pray to the Lord.

CHOIR: Lord, have mercy.

PRIEST: O Lord our God, who didst accompany the servant of the patriarch Abraham into Mesopotamia, when he was sent to espouse a wife for his lord Isaac, and who, by means of the drawing of water, didst reveal to him that he should betroth Rebecca: Do Thou, the same Lord, bless also the betrothal of these Thy servants, [*name*] and [*name*], and confirm the promise that they have made. Establish them in the holy union which is from Thee. For in the beginning Thou didst make them male and female, and by Thee the woman is joined unto the man as a helper and for the procreation of the human race. Therefore, O Lord our God, who hast sent forth Thy truth upon Thine inheritance, and Thy covenant unto Thy servants our fathers, Thine elect from generation to generation: Look upon Thy servant, [*name*], and Thy handmaiden, [*name*], and establish and make firm their betrothal, in faith and in oneness of mind, in truth and in love. For Thou, O Lord, hast declared that a pledge should be given and confirmed in all things. By a ring power was given to Joseph in Egypt; by a ring Daniel was glorified in the land of Babylon; by a ring the uprightness of Tamar was revealed; by a ring our heavenly Father showed His bounty upon His Son, for He said: Bring the fatted calf and kill it, and let us eat and make merry. By Thine own right hand, O Lord, Thou didst arm Moses in the Red Sea; by Thy true word the heavens were established, and the foundations of the earth were made firm; and the right hands of Thy servants also shall be blessed by Thy mighty word and by Thine upraised arm. Therefore, O Master, bless now this putting-on of rings with Thy heavenly blessing, and let Thine angel go before them all the days of their life. For Thou art He that blesses and sanctifies all things, and unto Thee are due all glory, honor, and worship: to the Father, and to the Son, and to the Holy Spirit, now and ever and unto ages of ages.

CHOIR: Amen.

The couple is betrothed in the name of the Father, Son, and Holy Spirit. To be blessed in the name of the Trinity puts us in the grace or power of the Trinity. The name of God has power in itself. Remember how those who came to arrest Jesus in the garden of Gethsemane responded to Jesus' identification of himself: "As soon then as he had said unto them, 'I am [he]' [see Ex 3.14], they went backward, and fell to the ground" (Jn 18.6). God's name allows us to experience God's action in our lives. Christ told us that whatever we ask the Father in his name, the Father will do (Jn 14.13). The life of the Holy Trinity is the greatest expression of love. God gives marriage as a life-giving gift, allowing human life to be joined to that of the Trinity. Here we can say that marriage reflects the life of God. In the Orthodox marriage rite, there is no exchange of vows, because we emphasize what God is doing in marriage. Nevertheless, couples dream and plan together during their courtship and share with each other their hopes and aspirations. In this prayer we ask God "to confirm the promise that they have made," which, as Fr Schmemann emphasized to his students, includes all of the words and dreams shared by the couple that are unto salvation. We do not, however, ask the couple to share these intimate feelings and dreams with their coworkers, families, and friends in such a public forum.

Each reference to rings in this ritual shows God working in the lives of his people. God traveled with Abraham's servant to get a wife for Isaac; God in the beginning made man male and female; and so it is by God that we are connected to each other in marriage. God delivered Joseph and saved his family, God blesses couples with children, and God expresses forgiveness and joy. God, who gives each of us a guardian angel at baptism, is now asked to send a guardian angel to protect this marriage, which is from him. Couples are reminded that a guardian accompanies them, from whom they can draw support to choose well and be delivered from evil ones and the temptations of the fallen world.[4] In other words, along with your baptismal angels, you and your spouse are given an additional angel to protect your marriage.

PRIEST: Blessed is every one who fears the Lord, who walks in His ways.

CHOIR: Glory to Thee, our God, glory to Thee! *(Refrain)*

The term here translated as "blessed" also means "holy," "happy," "satisfied," and "content." In this context the word "blessed" carries all of these connotations. Those who fear the Lord or who stand in awe of God with deference and respect are those who are aware of our appropriate relationship with God. We walk in his ways or,

[4]See Genesis 24.30 for more about angels being with us.

speaking more precisely, we respond to God's love for us and his presence with us; we love him back and follow him. When we stand with God, all that is created will see and should acknowledge his glory. When we glorify God, we venerate him. This is a totally reasonable response—or even the only reasonable response. If we do not glorify God, we repeat the sin of Adam, which is to seek to be our own god, ignoring God and his command.

PRIEST: You shall eat of the fruit of the labor of your hands; you shall be happy, and it shall be well with you.

Not everything that we do brings the expected or desired rewards. When we work righteously, we hope to be blessed, but good and bad things happen to everyone. "That you may be the children of your Father who is in heaven: for he makes his sun to rise on the evil and on the good, and sends rain on the just and on the unjust" (Mt 5.45). It is a blessing when you work hard and get good results. It certainly makes sense to work hard, and good results often follow, but not expecting anything allows us to simply be content, while expectations always leave us wanting. This is because what we get can never match the expectations of our imagination. Being content is an attitude that allows more contentment, while discontent breeds discontent.

PRIEST: Your wife will be like a fruitful vine upon the walls of your house; Your children will be like olive shoots around your table.

The analogy of a wife being like a fruitful vine upon the walls of one's house is rich with images of life. The grape vine produces grapes to be turned into wine, which is a symbol of life. Furthermore, the abundance of fruit that can come from a single vine is a symbol of the wife as a bearer of children and source of abundant joy. The walls allow for us to be protected from all that is outside, support the roof that shelters us, and offer a boundary for the purpose of security.

Olive oil was the only fat that could be stored for the winter in ancient Israel, so it served many functions. It was an important food, the only medicine for closing wounds, makeup for brightening faces, and a source of light to study with in the evening, and it was used ritualistically to anoint kings, prophets, and priests. It takes many olives to produce oil, and many kinds of olives come from trees with thorns. A newly planted olive orchard is an archetypal image of hope, because conquering armies would deprive populations of olive oil to weaken them. Due to this, olive trees would only be planted if peace was expected in the future, because it takes many years for olive trees to produce any fruit. When we plant olive trees it is not a work for us, but for our children. We have olive trees and know the joy of their fruit only if our parents planted them for us. Olive oil is greatly valued, is produced with hard work, and is part of almost every aspect of life. What joy it is to have a wife and children like a newly planted olive orchard!

PRIEST: Lo, thus shall the man be blessed who fears the Lord. The Lord bless you from Zion! May you see the prosperity of Jerusalem all the days of your life! May you see your children's children! Peace be upon Israel!

The purpose of uniting the bride and groom is for this union to bring the couple into a partnership that leads them to salvation and allows them to have children, which they raise in a little church, the family. In Revelation 3.12 Jerusalem and Zion are images of salvation, calling for the married couple to unite their family to the Church: "Him that overcomes will I make a pillar in the temple of my God, and he shall go no more out: and I will write upon him the name of my God, and the name of the city of my God, which is new Jerusalem, which comes down out of heaven from my God: and I will write upon him my new name." This image is that of the Church at liturgy, and the family is a little church, which supports the Church and is supported by it. Both are for the salvation of God's people.

With this transition complete, we are now coming to the start of this sacramental service. Like all liturgy, the church gathers in Christ's name to make manifest the kingdom of God, which we say is in the body of Christ. This is a mystical reality expressing God's time and place. We have now set behind our earthly cares, and God acts in his own time and space. This is captured in the *kairos* (καιρός), or time, when the deacon comes and calls the bishop or priest to "bless," for it is the time for God to act. The priest lifts the Gospel Book or traces the censer over the Gospel Book, proclaiming that the kingdom of God the Father, Son, and Holy Spirit is blessed. This shows that marriage takes place in the kingdom; similarly, in the liturgy the Eucharist is received in the kingdom.

PRIEST: Blessed is the Kingdom of the Father, and of the Son, and of the Holy Spirit, now and ever and unto ages of ages.

CHOIR: Amen.

We now repeat some of the petitions that were prayed in the betrothal service:

PRIEST: In peace let us pray to the Lord.

CHOIR: Lord, have mercy.

PRIEST: For the peace from above and for the salvation of our souls, let us pray to the Lord.

CHOIR: Lord, have mercy.

PRIEST: For the peace of the whole world, for the welfare of the holy churches of God, and for the union of all, let us pray to the Lord.

CHOIR: Lord, have mercy.

PRIEST: For this holy house and for those who enter with faith, reverence, and the fear of God, let us pray to the Lord.

CHOIR: Lord, have mercy.

PRIEST: For His Beatitude, our Metropolitan [*name*], and for His (Eminence, Grace), our (Archbishop, Bishop) [*name*], for the honorable priesthood, the diaconate in Christ, for all the clergy and the people, let us pray to the Lord.

CHOIR: Lord, have mercy.

PRIEST: For the servants of God, [*name*] and [*name*], who are now being united to each other in the community of marriage, and for their salvation, let us pray to the Lord.

CHOIR: Lord, have mercy.

The Church prays for the couple that is now being united to each other in the community of marriage. There is a resistance to pronouncing a couple married, or to defining when precisely the couple is married. God is acting in marriage, so it is not up to us to say when and how he works. Marriage is a way of life, which is about sharing and working in God together. Marriage is a gift from above and a oneness that cannot be reduced to the pronouncement by a person, be that person a clergyman or the couple themselves. We also suggest that a couple that has shared fifty years of a common life are sharing it differently than that couple did on their first dance on their wedding day. Our point is that God is acting in our lives, and as this petition suggests, he is acting for our salvation.

PRIEST: That He will bless this marriage, as he blessed the marriage in Cana of Galilee, let us pray to the Lord.

CHOIR: Lord, have mercy.

Christ blessed the wedding feast by his presence. Just as Christ was present at the wedding in Cana of Galilee, so he will be present at our weddings. When the people at the feast had run out of wine, Mary interceded before Christ. By doing so, Mary spared the hosts embarrassment. Christ took the water for ritual purification and showed it to be life-giving wine. As we noted earlier,[5] at the time of Christ, most water was not suitable for drinking, as standing water was exposed to disease and pollutants. When water was poured into the vineyard, it was filtered first by the ground and then by the grape vines. The alcohol in wine, which is made from grapes, killed germs and made wine a beverage that was safer to drink than unfiltered standing water. Wine was therefore an essential drink that supported life. Not only was the water meant for washing at Cana made wine, but this wine was the finest wine. God takes our earthly gifts and returns them as heavenly. He takes what is of the fallen world and uses it to manifest his presence and his kingdom. The fact that Christ chose to take wine, a sign of life, and use it to manifest his life or blood in the Eucharist cannot be overlooked here. Like the Eucharist, marriage is about salvation and the kingdom.

[5]See pp. 58–59.

PRIEST: That He will grant to them chastity, and of the fruit of the womb as is expedient for them, let us pray to the Lord.

CHOIR: Lord, have mercy.

Not everything that is pleasurable is holy or good. Everything should be used well and for its intended purpose. The marriage bed is about selfless love. The icon of the conception of the Theotokos captures such gentleness, attentiveness, and tenderness: Joachim and Anna are listening to each other, communing beyond words. They are sharing and giving in a way that expresses love. With God they produce a pure and holy child, who will open the way of salvation for the world. This is not selfish, violent, dominant, or about human ecstasy. This icon reflects the oneness of God that we are created to share in.

PRIEST: That he will make them glad with the sight of sons and daughters, let us pray to the Lord.

CHOIR: Lord, have mercy.

Some people are aware that their selfishness precludes sharing their life with children and are able to articulate that. Others compete with their children for the attention of their spouse and others in their lives. When their basic needs are met, most people mature to a level that allows them to meet their own needs and share their love with children. This takes practice and a good attitude. The Church can be a place where our immaturities are challenged, our skills are developed, and holistic living is promoted.

PRIEST: That He will grant to them enjoyment of the blessing of children, and a blameless life, let us pray to the Lord.

CHOIR: Lord, have mercy.

Marriage creates new families that are meant to be little churches where children learn to become healthy citizens. Citizenship in a secular society promotes good church citizenship, and good church citizenship models citizenship in the secular society. We belong to the Church, but also live in the world. As much as is possible, it is good to live harmoniously with others. Christians need to model good citizenship so that others can discover the God we worship. We cannot witness to the world if we are not peaceful, upright, and mature citizens. Christians would do well to teach their children to be good citizens of the society we live in as well as good witnesses to the God who is within us.

PRIEST: That He will grant to them and to us, all our petitions which are unto salvation, let us pray to the Lord.

CHOIR: Lord, have mercy.

PRIEST: That He will deliver them and us from all affliction, wrath, danger, and necessity, let us pray to the Lord.

CHOIR: Lord, have mercy.

PRIEST: Help us, save us, have mercy on us, and keep us, O God, by Thy grace.

CHOIR: Lord, have mercy.

PRIEST: Commemorating our most holy, most pure, most blessed and glorious Lady Theotokos and ever-virgin Mary with all the Saints, let us commend ourselves and each other, and all our life unto Christ our God.

CHOIR: To Thee, O Lord.

PRIEST: For unto Thee are due all glory, honor, and worship: to the Father, and to the Son, and to the Holy Spirit, now and ever and unto ages of ages.

CHOIR: Amen.

With the previous petitions, we have set before God our needs. In the following prayer, we now acknowledge that God has saved our spiritual forefathers and has been active in their lives and particularly in their marriages for their salvation. We ask God to bless this marriage as he blessed those of the forefathers. We notice that the forefathers were faithful to God, and God rewarded their faithfulness with children. We now address God, who created this bride and groom in their respective parents' families, to now ask him to bless and create a new family. We now come to the first marriage prayer.

PRIEST: Let us pray to the Lord.

CHOIR: Lord, have mercy.

Then the priest recites aloud the following prayer:

PRIEST: O God most pure, fashioner of every creature, who didst transform the rib of our forefather Adam into a wife, because of Thy love towards mankind, and didst bless them and say to them: Be fruitful and multiply, and fill the earth and subdue it; who didst make of the two one flesh: Therefore a man leaves his father and his mother and cleaves to his wife, and the two shall become one flesh, and what God has joined together, let no man put asunder: Thou didst bless Thy servant Abraham, and opening the womb of Sarah didst make him to be the father of many nations. Thou didst give Isaac to Rebecca, and didst bless her in childbearing. Thou didst join Jacob unto Rachel, and from them didst bring forth the twelve patriarchs. Thou didst unite Joseph and Aseneth, giving to them Ephraim and Manasseh as the fruit of their procreation. Thou didst accept Zechariah and Elizabeth, and didst make their offspring to be the Forerunner. From the root of Jesse according to the flesh, Thou didst bud forth the ever-virgin one, and wast incarnate of her, and wast born of her for the redemption of the human race. Through Thine unutterable gift and manifold goodness, Thou didst come to Cana of Galilee, and didst bless the marriage there, to make manifest that it is Thy will that there should be lawful marriage and procreation. Do Thou, the same all-holy Master, accept the prayers of us Thy servants. As Thou wast present there, be Thou also present here, with Thine invisible protection. Bless this marriage, and grant to these Thy servants, [*name*] and [*name*], a peaceful life, length of days, chastity, mutual love in the bond of peace, long-lived offspring, gratitude from their children, a crown of glory that does not fade away. Graciously grant that they may see their children's children. Preserve their bed unassailed, and give them of the dew of heaven from on high, and of the fatness of the earth. Fill their houses with wheat, wine, and oil and with every good thing, so that they may give in turn to those in need; and grant also to those here present with them all those petitions which are for their salvation. For Thou art the God of mercies, and of bounties, and of love towards mankind, and unto Thee we ascribe glory: to the Father, and to the Son, and to the Holy Spirit, now and ever and unto ages of ages.

CHOIR: Amen.

The Genesis creation narrative is very important for us to understand here, because it sets out the Orthodox perspective of our relationship with God and how men and women are to relate to each other. God creates everything, and all of it is meant to be orderly and functional. The crown of this creation is man, who is in the image and likeness of God. Now, if man had been created last, after woman, woman would be part of creation for man's service. Likewise, if woman had been created last, after man, man would be in her service. In the Genesis account, man is created last, but woman comes from his side or his rib. The formula is brilliant! Woman is of equal substance as man and is neither above nor below him (Gen 2.21). Together they will form a family and God is asked to bless them by meeting all of the earthly needs that they will have. He is also asked to grant them a life in holiness and that they will follow God. Note here that God gives us abundant gifts so that as stewards we can take care of the poor and each other. In so doing we share in God's own care of his world.

PRIEST: Let us pray to the Lord.

CHOIR: Lord, have mercy.

Then the priest recites aloud the following prayer:

PRIEST: Blessed art Thou, O Lord our God, Priest of mystical and undefiled marriage, and ordainer of the law of the marriage of the body; preserver of immortality, and provider of the good things of life; the same master who in the beginning didst make man and establish him as a king over creation, and didst say: "It is not good that man should be alone upon the earth. Let us make a helper fit for him." Taking one of his ribs, Thou didst fashion woman; and when Adam saw her he said: "This is at last bone of my bones and flesh of my flesh; she shall be called Woman, because she was taken out of Man." For this reason a man shall leave his father and mother and be joined to his wife, and the two shall become one flesh; what therefore God has joined together, let no man put asunder: Do Thou now also, O Master, our Lord and our God, send down Thy heavenly grace upon these Thy servants, [*name*] and [*name*]; grant that this Thy handmaiden may be subject to her husband in all things, and that this Thy servant may be the head of his wife, so that they may live according to Thy will. Bless them, O Lord our God, as Thou didst bless Abraham and Sarah. Bless them, O Lord our God, as Thou didst bless Isaac and Rebecca. Bless them, O Lord our God, as Thou didst bless Jacob and all the patriarchs. Bless them, O Lord our God, as Thou didst bless Joseph and Aseneth. Bless them, O Lord our God, as Thou didst bless Moses and Zipporah. Bless them, O Lord our God, as Thou didst bless Joachim and Anna. Bless them, O Lord our God, as Thou didst bless Zechariah and Elizabeth. Preserve them, O Lord our God, as Thou didst preserve Noah in the Ark. Preserve them, O Lord our God, as Thou didst preserve Jonah in the belly of the whale. Preserve them, O Lord our God, as Thou didst preserve the three holy children from the fire, sending down upon them dew from heaven; and let that gladness come upon them which the blessed Helen had when she found the precious cross. Remember them, O Lord our God, as Thou didst remember Enoch, Shem, Elijah. Remember them, O Lord our God, as Thou didst remember Thy forty holy martyrs, sending down upon them crowns from heaven. Remember them, O Lord our God, and the parents who have nurtured them, for the prayers of parents make firm the foundations of houses. Remember, O Lord our God, Thy servants, the groomsman and the bridesmaid of the bridal pair, who have come together in this joy. Remember, O Lord our God, Thy servant, [*name*], and Thy handmaiden, [*name*], and bless them. Grant them of the fruit of their bodies, fair children, concord of soul and body. Exalt them like the cedars of Lebanon, like a luxuriant vine. Give them offspring in number like unto full ears of grain; so that, having enough of all things, they may abound in every work that is good and acceptable unto Thee. Let them see their children's children, like olive shoots around their table; so that, finding favor in Thy sight, they may shine like the stars of heaven, in Thee our God. For unto Thee are due all glory, honor, and worship: to the Father, and to the Son, and to the Holy Spirit, now and ever and unto ages of ages.

CHOIR: Amen.

This prayer is rich with imagery and invitations to live a Christian lifestyle, which are very helpful to examine. God is addressed as the Priest of mystical and pure marriage. Also declared is that God established marriage to help us work out our salvation, and that he has ordered the world in such a way that marriages may produce children. Ordination is used to recognize a vocation or lifelong commitment. The couple is ordained to be a church where the family worships God and sanctifies time and space. After these bold statements, we are taught why God has given men and women to each other. It is good for us to be in community and not alone. Just as God is not alone, so we also are to have each other. This is such a sacred gift that God ordains that it should be respected and preserved pure. So they are no longer two but one flesh. "What therefore God has joined together, let not man put asunder" (Mt 19.6).

Through this gift we are also called to leave our family of origin and cleave to one another, making a new family. This is not easy for many Orthodox. Some traditionally Orthodox lands tend to be matriarchal, where husbands and sons are taught to take care of and give deference to the matriarch. Women of these cultures are accustomed to taking care of the extended family and coordinating all family events and relationships. Because their service is to the family, they are in fact the leaders. How terrible indeed it is for a man to be caught between a mother and a wife. It is comparable to being tortured by having one's arms tied to two horses moving in different directions. The solution to this age-old dilemma is beyond our competency and the scope of this reflection; however, we will point out that our wedding ritual follows the scriptural calling for a man to "leave his father and his mother and . . . cleave unto his wife" (Gen 2.24).

Professor Veselin Kesich (of blessed memory) discovered that the term "head" used in Ephesians 5 (and in this prayer) is referencing Genesis,[6] implying that man is the source of the woman.[7] Again, the term "source" is used to show equality of substance, rather than inferiority of being. If man had been created last, then woman, like all of that which is created, would be created for his use. If woman had been created last, then man would be for her pleasure. The genius of the creation story is that man is created last, and woman from his side, showing they are of equal substance yet maintain an order.

When parents pray for their married adult children, they hand them over to God and interfere less in their lives. Instead of judging their married adult children, they join them in seeking God's will and blessings. Sometimes new parents are bothered that grandparents spoil the children and do not follow all of the parents' rules when watching the children. We believe that children mostly develop their

---

[6]See Gen 2.23: "This at last is bone of my bones and flesh of my flesh; she shall be called Woman, because she was taken out of Man."

[7]"[W]e must mention that the head in Eph. 5, as well as in I Cor. 11, should not be interpreted in the sense of ruler, but in the sense of origin, of the beginning of something. As the Church has its origin in Christ, the woman has her origin in man. Here St. Paul does not speak of man as a ruler over his wife, but refers to the creation of woman in Gen. 2. She was made from man. Man is her 'head,' that is, origin." Veselin Kesich, "St. Paul: Anti-Feminist or Liberator?," *St Vladimir's Theological Quarterly* 21.3 (1977): 130–31.

understanding based on the way their own parents live, and that they are influenced much less by grandparents, aunts and uncles, and the friends of their parents. Children have a capacity to learn different languages; likewise, they can learn different rules for their home, their grandparents' house, and other places without difficulty. We would do well to overlook all but the most critical things.

We ask God to bless us as he blessed those forefathers, whom God made his own through his covenant and whom he blessed with spouses and children. We then ask God to protect us as he did Noah by the ark. The Church is built to be a kind of ark that protects its passengers from the storms of tribulation, which reign outside. The church building is even built like an ark, and to this day often features round windows or portals.

We ask God to exalt the couple like cedars of Lebanon. These trees, which are thousands of years old and enormous, seem to reach for the sky straight out of the mountains. Unlike other cedar trees, these trees hold their branches horizontally to the ground, in the same position that the ancient Jews assumed as they prayed—with arms outstretched. When King David saw them, he called them "the trees of the Lord," since they seemed to be exalting God.[8] The married couple ought to become like a luxuriant vine, which gives abundant life. Remember that without the fruit of the vine, ancient man would have become dehydrated because standing water was polluted with disease. The married couple are likewise to shine like the stars of heaven. Furthermore, "children's children are the crown of old men; and the glory of children are their fathers" (Prov 17.6; see also Deut 5.16).

PRIEST: Let us pray to the Lord.

CHOIR: Lord, have mercy.

[8]See Is 14.8 and Ps 104.16.

And again the priest prays aloud:

PRIEST: O holy God, who didst form man from the dust, and didst fashion woman from his rib, and didst join her unto him as a helper, for it seemed good to Thy majesty that man should not be alone upon the earth: Do Thou, the same Lord, stretch out now also Thy hand from Thy holy dwelling-place, and unite this Thy servant, [*name*], and this Thy handmaiden, [*name*]; for by Thee is the husband joined unto the wife. Unite them in one mind; wed them into one flesh, granting to them the fruit of the body and the procreation of fair children. For Thine is the majesty, and Thine is the Kingdom and the power and the glory: of the Father, and of the Son, and of the Holy Spirit, now and ever and unto ages of ages.

CHOIR: Amen.

God creates man out of the dust of the earth: that is to say, we are creatures, and not of the same substance as God. Although we are made in his image and can share in his life by adoption, we are not God. God, who makes us male and female, brings us together in marriage to be one flesh and share in his creation. God creates, and people procreate. God joins husband and wife, making them *complete*, and calls them to support each other. "Complete" means that, since God is love, the wife's love for her husband and the husband's love for his wife make them more reflective of God the Father, who loves the Son and Holy Spirit from all eternity. Christians who are not yet married or who live in parish or monastic communities are also called to love, but their love is expressed differently from those who are made one in marriage.

The priest takes the crowns, which recall those with which the "martyrs," or witnesses of Christ, are crowned in heaven, and crowns first the bridegroom, saying:

PRIEST: The servant of God, [*name*], is crowned unto the handmaiden of God, [*name*], In the name of the Father, and of the Son, and of the Holy Spirit.

So also he crowns the bride, saying:

PRIEST: The handmaiden of God, [*name*], is crowned unto the servant of God, [*name*], In the name of the Father, and of the Son, and of the Holy Spirit.

Then he blesses them three times, saying each time:

PRIEST: O Lord our God, crown them with glory and honor.

The crowns are explained in Part Two of this book,[9] but we wish to point out here that the term "crown" is sometimes understood as "glory." A virtuous wife is the "crown" or "glory" of her husband, and a holy husband is the crown of his wife. Again the crowns show martyrdom, stewardship, and victory over sin. Crowning is a kind of ordination or rite of passage, a solidifying of their marriage and of their new household.

PRIEST: Let us attend. Peace be unto all.

READER: And to your spirit.

PRIEST: Wisdom!

[9] See pp. 49–58.

99

READER: The Prokeimenon in the eighth tone. *(Psalm 21):* Thou hast set upon their heads crowns of precious stones; they asked life of Thee, and Thou gavest it them.

VERSE: Yea, Thou wilt make them most blessed for ever; Thou wilt make them glad with the joy of Thy presence.

The *prokeimenon* offers us the themes of the scriptural lessons to be heard from the psalms. The lessons of marriage and the Scripture readings are about God's blessing, about joy, about value, about life and salvation.

PRIEST: Wisdom!

READER: The reading from the Epistle of the holy Apostle Paul to the Ephesians.

PRIEST: Let us attend.

READER: *(Eph 5.20–33)* Brethren: Give thanks always and for everything in the name of our Lord Jesus Christ to God the Father. Be subject to one another out of reverence for Christ. Wives, be subject to your husbands, as to the Lord. For the husband is head of the wife as Christ is head of the church, His body, and is Himself its Savior. As the Church is subject to Christ, so let wives also be subject in everything to their husbands. Husbands, love your wives, as Christ loved the Church and gave Himself up for her, so that He might sanctify her, having cleansed her by the washing of water with the word, that the Church might be presented before Him in splendor, without spot or wrinkle or any such thing, that she might be holy and without blemish. Even so husbands should love their wives as their own bodies. He who loves his wife loves himself. For no man ever hates his own flesh, but nourishes and cherishes it, as Christ does the Church, because we are members of His body. "For this reason a man shall leave his father and mother and be joined to his wife, and the two shall become one." This is a great mystery, and I take it to mean Christ and the Church; however, let each one of you love his wife as himself and let the wife see that she respects her husband.

PRIEST: Peace be unto you, reader.

READER: And to your spirit. Alleluia! Alleluia! Alleluia!

Note that the last two sentences of the reading offer us some insights about this epistle. This letter of St Paul to the people of Ephesus is about the relationship of Christ and his Church, which is reflected in the intimate relationship between husband and wife. After the lesson, St Paul takes the opportunity to exhort husbands and wives to love and respect each other. This is such an important and vital part of marriage; in counseling, we have never seen a couple in trouble who felt cherished and respected by each other.

The chapter opens with the bold statement: "Give thanks always and for everything in the name of our Lord Jesus Christ to God the Father. Be subject to one another out of reverence for Christ." When a couple is right with God, they are following God, wanting what God wants for themselves and each other. The couple is building the kingdom of heaven in their marriage. It is in this context that we obey one another, because our spouse is the one who will bring us to Christ for salvation. Husbands are to care for the needs of their wives. If a husband is cold, he should give his wife a coat. If he is hungry, he should provide food. If a wife needs something, she should meet her husband's needs as well. This epistle uses the word "head" here, which ought be understood in reference to Genesis, as we have discussed above, showing that St Paul is using the creation narrative to explain our relationships with God and each other. We share the same humanity and are joined by God to each other, so we ought to care for and love each other. When some misinterpret this part of Scripture and complain that it favors the authority of men over women, we are quick to point out that while women are called to obey their husbands, men are called to die for their wives as Christ sacrificed himself for us and his Church.

PRIEST: Peace be unto all.

CHOIR: And to your spirit.

PRIEST: The reading from the Holy Gospel according to Saint John.

CHOIR: Glory to Thee, O Lord, glory to Thee.

PRIEST: Let us attend.

(Jn 2.1–11) In those days there was a wedding at Cana in Galilee, and the mother of Jesus was there; Jesus also was invited to the marriage, with His disciples. When the wine failed, the mother of Jesus said to Him, "They have no wine." And Jesus said to her, "O woman, what have you to do with me? My hour has not yet come." His mother said to the servants, "Do whatever He tells you." Now six stone jars were standing there, for the Jewish rites of purification, each holding twenty or thirty gallons. Jesus said to them, "Fill the jars with water." And they filled them up to the brim. He said to them, "Now draw some out, and take it to the steward of the feast." So they took it. When the steward of the feast tasted the water now become wine, and did not know where it came from (though the servants who had drawn the water knew), the steward of the feast called the bridegroom and

said to him, "Every man serves the good wine first; and when men have drunk freely, then the poor wine; but you have kept the good wine until now." This, the first of his signs, Jesus did at Cana in Galilee, and manifested His glory; and His disciples believed in Him.

CHOIR: Glory to Thee, O Lord, glory to Thee.

On the third day of creation, God created land, separated the waters, and brought forth vegetation (Gen 1.9). On the third day after the crucifixion, Christ rose from the dead, fulfilling the prophecies of the Scriptures. Between these two events, beginning his earthly ministry on the third day of the week, Jesus went to Cana of Galilee and performed his first miracle (Jn 2.1). The act of marriage was understood to join a new family to their land, which they were to be stewards over. Taking the water of the Jewish rites of purification, Christ blesses and then makes this water the best of wine. Wine is once again a basic symbol of life, as it was the safest beverage to drink in the ancient world. God celebrates at the wedding with the couple and shares himself with them.

The role of Mary as intercessor is an important component of this Gospel reading. Mary came to Jesus with the embarrassment of the couple—the fact that the wine had run out. Many think that the wedding in Cana was for a relative of Mary. Popular Orthodox tradition names Simon the Zealot as the groom.[11] When the couple were in need of more wine, Mary interceded with her Son. Because she is the mother of Jesus, she does have a special role in his life, and therefore also in salvation history. Jesus called her "woman," which may be heard by modern ears as suspicious or disrespectful, but that

---

[10]E.g., *The Lives of the Holy Apostles*, Rdr. Isaac Lambertson, trans. (Buena Vista, CO: Holy Apostles Convent, 1990), 229. [This life of St Simon was written by St Dimitri of Rostov in the late seventeenth century.—*Ed.*]

is reading something of modern culture into an entirely different context. We do not consider being called "man" to be necessarily derogatory today; "woman" or "lady" is in the above context a title of respect.

In an effort to define themselves as "non-Roman Catholic," some Protestants have become excessively sensitive to anything that looks "Roman Catholic." The veneration of Mary and the saints has unfortunately been lost to those of the Reformed tradition. Mary said "yes" to God, and salvation is possible by the incarnation that she accepted to be accomplished through her. Some debate what could or would have happened had Mary refused. Such discussion is merely hypothetical, because Mary did say "yes." For the Orthodox, Mary is a great example of Christian life. She said "yes" to God, and she is saved by him. As members of our Church, she and the saints are supporters and witnesses of our own Christian lives. They pray for us. Just as we pray for and love each other within the Church, so we also commune with those who are alive in Christ, though they have lived in other generations.

The Litany of Fervent Supplication

In the litany of fervent supplication, we set forth the petitions that are foremost on our hearts as we gather.

PRIEST: Let us all say with all our soul and with all our mind, let us say.

CHOIR: Lord, have mercy.

PRIEST: O Lord almighty, the God of our fathers, we pray Thee, hearken and have mercy.

CHOIR: Lord, have mercy.

PRIEST: Have mercy on us, O God, according to Thy great goodness, we pray Thee, hearken and have mercy.

CHOIR: Lord, have mercy. (3)

PRIEST: Again we pray for mercy, life, peace, health, salvation, and visitation for the servants of God, [*name*] and [*name*] (and he mentions also whomever else he wishes), and for the pardon and remission of their sins.

CHOIR: Lord, have mercy. (3)

Note that in this petition the bride and groom are prayed for together as the servants of God. Previously in the service they were prayed for separately as "the servant of God and the handmaiden of God."

PRIEST: For Thou art a merciful God, and lovest mankind, and unto Thee we ascribe glory: to the Father, and to the Son, and to the Holy Spirit, now and ever and unto ages of ages.

CHOIR: Amen.

PRIEST: Let us pray to the Lord.

CHOIR: Lord, have mercy.

PRIEST: O Lord our God, who in Thy saving dispensation didst vouchsafe by Thy presence in Cana of Galilee to declare marriage honorable: Do Thou, the same Lord, now also maintain in peace and concord Thy servants, [*name*] and [*name*], whom Thou hast been pleased to join together. Cause their marriage to be honorable. Preserve their bed blameless. Mercifully grant that they may live together in purity; and enable them to reach a ripe old age, walking in Thy commandments with a pure heart. For

Thou art our God, the God of mercy and salvation, and unto Thee we ascribe glory: to the Father, and to the Son, and to the Holy Spirit, now and ever and unto ages of ages.

CHOIR: Amen.

God has ordered the world in such a way that everyone has all that they need to have eternal life. God could have put us in different lands or different centuries, but by his providence, God has ordered the world in such a way that we may find each other and come to this day. It is of course our own choice to marry; God did not force us to marry, but has given us these opportunities to come together and make free choices.

The Litany before the Lord's Prayer

PRIEST: Help us, save us, have mercy on us, and keep us, O God, by Thy grace.

CHOIR: Lord, have mercy.

PRIEST: That the whole day may be perfect, holy, peaceful, and sinless, let us ask of the Lord.

CHOIR: Grant it, O Lord.

PRIEST: An angel of peace, a faithful guide, a guardian of our souls and bodies, let us ask of the Lord.

CHOIR: Grant it, O Lord.

PRIEST: Pardon and remission of our sins and transgressions, let us ask of the Lord.

CHOIR: Grant it, O Lord.

PRIEST: All things that are good and profitable for our souls, and peace for the world, let us ask of the Lord.

CHOIR: Grant it, O Lord.

PRIEST: That we may complete the remaining time of our life in peace and repentance, let us ask of the Lord.

CHOIR: Grant it, O Lord.

PRIEST: A Christian ending to our life: painless, blameless, and peaceful; and a good defense before the dread judgment seat of Christ, let us ask of the Lord.

CHOIR: Grant it, O Lord.

PRIEST: Having asked for the unity of the Faith, and communion of the Holy Spirit, let us commend ourselves and each other, and all our life unto Christ our God.

CHOIR: To Thee, O Lord.

PRIEST: And make us worthy, O Master, that with boldness and without condemnation we may dare to call on Thee, the heavenly God, as Father, and to say:

The Lord's Prayer

CHOIR: Our Father, who art in heaven, hallowed be Thy name. Thy Kingdom come. Thy will be done, on earth as it is in heaven. Give us this day our daily bread; and forgive us our trespasses, as we forgive those who trespass against us; and lead us not into temptation, but deliver us from evil.

PRIEST: For Thine is the Kingdom, and the power, and the glory: of the Father, and of the Son, and of the Holy Spirit, now and ever and unto ages of ages.

CHOIR: Amen.

Only in Christ can we call upon God as "Father" or "Abba" as we do in Christ's own prayer. But by God's choice, and by our being initiated into Christ in baptism, we now have boldness to come before God as sons and daughters. From within Christ, we call upon the Father to give us essential life, which is our daily bread, and to share his life, furthering his kingdom "on earth as it is in heaven." In Romans we understand that, now that we are sons by adoption, we ourselves are the first fruits of the Spirit (Rom 8.23). Our marriage is enveloped by God, who makes us one and who dwells in both husband and wife. When we share this unity, we naturally become inclined to call upon God as "Father" or "Abba."

The Prayer with Heads Bowed

PRIEST: Peace be unto all.

CHOIR: And to your spirit.

PRIEST: Bow your heads unto the Lord.

CHOIR: To Thee, O Lord.

Submitting to God together is the attitude that makes for a successful marriage. When both husband and wife submit to God's will, what is there to disagree about? He gives us unity, meets all our needs, shares our joys and our sorrows, and loves us perfectly. Trust is always difficult, but by practice and by faithful submission to God, we can grow together in faith and in love. Your spouse is there so that you can learn to trust in God with and through him or her. Husbands and wives need not compete, but rather share in each other as one. We are on the same team and win or lose together. St

John Chrysostom, when preaching about marriage, explains that the only competition between husband and wife should be about who can better serve the other![11]

Then the common cup is brought and the priest blesses it.

PRIEST: Let us pray to the Lord.

CHOIR: Lord, have mercy.

PRIEST: O God, who hast created all things by Thy might, and hast made firm the world, and adornest the crown of all things that Thou hast made: Bless now, with Thy spiritual blessing, this common cup, which Thou dost give to those who are now united for the communion of marriage. For blessed is Thy name, and glorified is Thy Kingdom, of the Father, and of the Son, and of the Holy Spirit, now and ever and unto ages of ages.

CHOIR: Amen.

Then, taking the cup, the priest gives it to them three times.[12] (In some traditions the choir here sings the hymn "I will take the cup of salvation.")

God created everything, saw that it was good, and crowned it. Here, crowning is an act of recognizing the beauty and effectiveness of the world; the world is crowned with purpose. By crowning his creation, God shows it to be good and allows it to be utilized for good. With a common cup of the fruit of the luxurious vines, pointing to the Eucharist, God blesses those who are now united in the communion, or community, of marriage. The common cup is a symbol of the unity and work that the couple will accomplish together in

---

[11] See John Chrysostom, *Homilies on Ephesians* 20 (NPNF[1] 13:143–52).
[12] *The Sacrament of Matrimony*, 22.

Christ. They will share in all of the fruits of their labors, both good and bad. Together they will face the consequences of the fallen world as well as their own errors, and in Christ they will overcome them.

The procession around the Gospel Book is similar to the baptismal procession and the processions for ordinations to the diaconate, priesthood, and episcopacy. Though in a different order from that of ordination, the same hymns are sung as an indication of the transformation that will take place. This action shows that the gospel is central, and that God is giving the couple a pathway or vocation that leads to salvation. The candles remind us that Christ is the light that will lead us to the kingdom. Christ himself is "the Way, the Truth and the Life" (Jn 14.6). The circular path that the couple takes around the Gospel Book signifies eternity and perfection.

CHOIR: Rejoice, O Isaiah! A virgin is with child; and shall bear a Son, Emmanuel: He is both God and man; and Orient is His name; magnifying Him, we call the virgin blessed.

This procession is a liturgical dance expressing joy and thanksgiving. Isaiah prophesied that a virgin would give birth, and her offspring would be God with us, opening to us the way to salvation (see Is 7.14). It seems appropriate that Isaiah would dance for joy at our weddings as we join the couple in witnessing to Christ and putting our hope and trust in him.

CHOIR: O holy martyrs, who fought the good fight and have received your crowns: Entreat ye the Lord, that He will have mercy on our souls.

The martyrs dance with us as they also are witnesses to God. These men and women died in witnessing to Christ and the truth. The bride and groom represent these saints by putting on crowns of martyrdom. The bride and groom are today witnessing in front of their guests that God is real and that they have chosen to receive this gift of marriage and love from God. There will certainly be many times when they will be called upon to witness to their faith. In our post-Christian world, even simple things like prayer at restaurants, making the sign of the cross before eating at secular banquets, or daily conversation mentioning Christ can elicit hostile glances. By living as good Christians in a secular world, we prepare ourselves to support and share with others when people have needs. Those around us will sense that we have what they need by seeing how we live. This is the most effective opportunity to share the gospel.

CHOIR: Glory to Thee, O Christ God, the apostles' boast, the martyrs' joy, whose preaching was the consubstantial Trinity.

The married couple will also teach the gospel to their offspring and each other. They will teach the gospel by the way they live their lives at work. They will follow Christ all the days of their lives, so it is natural that the apostles should dance for joy as we join their company and continue their work.

Then, taking the crown of the bridegroom, the priest says:

PRIEST: Be exalted like Abraham, O Bridegroom, and be blessed like Isaac; and multiply like Jacob, walking in peace, and keeping God's commandments in righteousness.

Once again we ask God to bless and exalt us as he did our forefathers who were faithful. They were blessed with many children and fruitful in their work. In this way we are again reminded to walk in righteousness.[13]

[13]See Ps 47.9, Gen 26.12, 1 Chr 16.13, and Rom 8.4.

Then, taking the crown of the bride, the priest says:

[PRIEST:] And you, O Bride: Be exalted like Sarah, and exult like Rebecca, and multiply like Rachel; and rejoice in your husband, fulfilling the conditions of the law, for this is well-pleasing to God.

The priest removes the crowns, bestows on the couple a final blessing, and sends them forth in peace to preach the gospel and live Christian lives as a new family united in wedlock.

PRIEST: Let us pray to the Lord.

CHOIR: Lord, have mercy.

PRIEST: O God, our God, who didst come to Cana of Galilee, and didst bless there the marriage feast: Bless also these Thy servants, who through Thy good providence now are united in wedlock. Bless their goings out and their comings in. Fill their life with good things. Receive their crowns into Thy Kingdom,[15] preserving them spotless, blameless, and without reproach, unto ages of ages.

CHOIR: Amen.

After God is asked to bless the couple, we acknowledge again that marriage is possible through God's providence. The "goings out and comings in" refer to all of the work and life the couple will experience as they live their lives united as one. God is asked to

---

[14]Metropolitan Kallistos (Ware) speaks of marriage as the pathway of salvation; see Kallistos (Ware), foreword to *Marriage as a Path to Holiness: Lives of Married Saints*, by David Ford and Mary Ford, 2nd ed. (Waymart, PA: St. Tikhon's Monastery Press, 2013), ix–xi.

allow for our needs to be met and to help us live a life that brings salvation. The couple is now blessed with what is often called the "nuptial blessing," which calls upon the Trinity to bless them and give them many years and everything that they need to receive the promise of salvation.

Nuptial Blessing

PRIEST: May the Father, and the Son, and the Holy Spirit, the all-holy, consubstantial, and life-giving Trinity, one Godhead and one Kingdom, bless you; and grant you length of days, fair children, progress in life and faith; and fill you with all earthly good things, and make you worthy to enjoy the good things of the promise; through the prayers of the holy Theotokos and of all the saints.

CHOIR: Amen.

The Dismissal

PRIEST: Wisdom! Most holy Theotokos, save us!

CHOIR: More honorable than the Cherubim, and more glorious beyond compare than the Seraphim; without defilement you gave birth to God the Word: true Theotokos, we magnify you.

PRIEST: Glory to Thee, O Christ our God and our hope, glory to Thee.

CHOIR: Glory to the Father, and to the Son, and to the Holy Spirit, now and ever and unto ages of ages. Amen. Lord, have mercy. (3) Father, bless.

Priest: May He who by His presence in Cana of Galilee declared marriage to be honorable, Christ our true God, through the prayers of His most pure Mother; of the holy, glorious, and all-laudable apostles; of the holy, God-crowned kings Constantine and Helen, equal to the apostles; of the holy great martyr, Procopius; and of all the saints: have mercy on us and save us, for He is good and loves mankind.

CHOIR: Amen.

[*Then, in the Byzantine (i.e., non-Slavic) tradition:*

PRIEST: Through the prayers of our holy fathers, Lord Jesus Christ our God, have mercy upon us and save us.

CHOIR: Amen.]

The saints commemorated here all have been mentioned or alluded to in the ceremony. The Theotokos is both virgin and mother; the apostles danced with us as we proclaimed their faith, which they passed on to us; Constantine and Helen found joy in finding the true cross, which strengthens us and offers us an image of victory to encourage our faith; and the great martyr Procopius of Caesarea gained victory in battle and was converted by a vision of the cross.

The holy fathers that are called to pray for us are the bishops and presbyters who are leading our Church today. Being in a parish and under parish leadership, we are supported and blessed to embark on a healthy marriage. Confident that all these saints, the angels, the Mother of God, and the entire Church are all praying for this holy union to remain steadfast and holy, newlyweds are made ready to continue married life for all eternity.

PART IV

Helpful Thoughts for Strengthening Marriages to be Further Explored[1]

Flexibility

It is often said that the most important indicator of success in this age is flexibility. Our world is changing at an ever-accelerating rate, so those who are able to be flexible and adapt are predicted to have the most success. Love in marriage can allow us see selectively and choose what is most important, or simply tolerate and celebrate our differences and idiosyncrasies. Imagining that we can change another person, protect our spouses or children, or choose for them is pointless because we simply cannot. Control is ultimately only an illusion. We need to love, teach, share, and trust. None of these behaviors are innate or can be taken for granted. They must be cultivated through practice.

Once I was waiting for one of my sons to come out of half-day preschool at our local public elementary school.[2] There were about two hundred children in the school yard, with one recess monitor.

---

[1]Internet research or the self-help or relationship sections at a bookstore are fine places to start. Parish book clubs make for a fun way to support each other and have fun.

[2]This is a personal story of Bishop John.

All of the preschool parents or grandparents were lined up on the sidewalk behind the fence, waiting for the preschoolers to march through the chaos of the yard. After what seemed to be a long time, a retired school principal asked me if I knew what it took to be a successful recess monitor. I confessed that I did not. He then offered me a most valuable metaphor. He said, "The monitor can only see ten percent of what goes wrong in the yard. If she sees more than ten percent, the children will not get their needed recreation, and she will be ineffective and exhaust herself. If she sees less than ten percent, the children will not be safe. She needs to know which children can fight each other, which balls will lead children into the street and put them in harm's way, and when to blow her whistle and stop the yard's activity." This ten-percent rule is applicable everywhere. Husbands and wives need to choose which of their spouse's ideas should be challenged, which offensive actions of their children need to be disciplined, which comments of co-workers need to confronted, and what teachings of the pastor need to be clarified. If we over-function, we will exhaust ourselves; if we under-function, we will become frustrated. We need to learn to be wise by practicing self-control and thinking through our thoughts before speaking. Remember to see only ten percent of what goes on around you.

Sometimes we imagine that other people will judge us for what our friends or relatives say or do. While we agree that it is wise to choose companions who are morally like-minded, we don't think that we need to assume responsibility for the thoughts or words of our children, spouses, parents, or siblings. Clergy and parishioners, like husbands and wives, would do well to avoid trying to control the thoughts or words of each other. This always leads to anxiety and struggle. That is not to say that we can't sometimes positively influence each other, either by communicating information, modeling our responses to shared experiences, or by waiting for safe opportunities to share and listen to each other's feelings and responses. Likewise, people should take responsibility for their own relationships; they will not be judged for the thoughts of their parents or children.

My wife did not assume responsibility for my relationships with her family members and taught me not to assume responsibility for hers.[3] My children from a very early age had strong relationships with members of both our families of origin, which they maintained without our interference and often without our knowledge. I find this to be healthy and helpful. I learned early on that these other relationships did not challenge or replace my relationship to them as a parent, which I believe holds primary importance in the life of a child. As long as I was clear about my feelings and standards, the children could keep track of the rules and priorities of each extended family member and benefit from contrasting them with our own. They are, after all, exposed to the opinions and priorities portrayed on television, as well as those of school teachers, church members, Sunday school teachers, and clergy. Rather than trying to control how my siblings cared for my children when they were in their care, I would have done well to trust the children to understand my standards and maintain them in my home.

Love Languages

In his book *The Five Love Languages*,[4] Gary Chapman outlines five different ways to express and experience love, which he calls "love languages." These love languages are: gifts, quality time, words of affirmation, acts of service (devotion), and physical touch (intimacy). Each of us has a primary and secondary love language, which are

[3]Personal story of Bishop John.

[4]Gary D. Chapman, *The Five Love Languages: How to Express Heartfelt Commitment to Your Mate* (Chicago, IL: Northfield, 1995).

the ways that we would most like to receive love from our spouse. We are all social creatures and need to receive love. Chapman uses the metaphor of a "love tank" to explain how we store and use our love. While everyone uses all of the love languages to some degree, we would be more effective if we showed our spouses love in their own love language, rather than showing it through our own love language. Chapman writes that people should not use the love languages that they like the most, but rather the love languages that their loved ones can best receive. Chapman suggests that to discover a love language, one must observe the way the other expresses love and analyze what he or she complains about most often. Chapman suggests that our love languages do not change over time, but instead develop and need to be nurtured in different ways.

There are quizzes online that might help you discover each other's love languages. We think that this activity would be worthwhile.

Communication between Men and Women Is Transcultural

In her book *You Just Don't Understand*,[5] Deborah Tannen, a professor of sociolinguistics at Georgetown University, writes that men and women think and understand the world so differently that all communication between them is transcultural. From childhood, boys and girls learn different approaches to language and communication. Females engage in "rapport-talk," a communication style meant to promote social affiliation and emotional connection, while males engage in "report-talk," a style focused on exchanging information with little emotional import. The differences, as Tannen shows, result in regular misunderstandings between men and women.

[5]Deborah Tannen, *You Just Don't Understand: Women and Men in Conversation* (New York: Ballantine, 1990).

When a woman meets her man after work, she wants to connect with him to share the events of the day. She wants him to appreciate and understand her. She wants him to connect with her and appreciate how hard she works. She wants to share herself. The man wants to give his wife his perspective on what she brings to him, because he mistakenly thinks that she is bringing him problems to fix. After all, that is what men do: they fix things. He offers gift after gift of how she could have done things differently to make life easier and more efficient. She hears his gifts as criticism and put-downs. She gets quiet and withdraws. He gets angry that she is angry and feels accused, misunderstood, and unappreciated. He was just trying to help.

Men, when your lady wants advice, she will ask for it. Otherwise, assume that she simply wants to share her thoughts, and you only need to listen and offer feedback to let her know that you are listening. Saying something like, "That must have made you feel . . ." or, "How insensitive of her to have done that," is sufficient for listening and connecting. Don't fix your wife. Cherish her and show her that you understand how important she is. Men, ladies need to be cherished by their man. St Paul reminds us of this in Ephesians 5.

Ladies, men are very fragile. They need to know you notice everything that they do: every dish they rinse and every toilet seat they lower. They need to feel respected and appreciated. They can't stand thinking that you are angry with them or don't recognize all they do. Making you happy is actually extremely important to them. Don't think that men are mind readers. They need to be reminded, and when you tell them what to do and they do it, give them credit for it and let it count. Never say, "It doesn't count if I have to tell you."

What to Do When Disagreeing

I find that people often seem to be disagreeing even when they are saying the same thing. When you hear something that seems off, check to be sure that the message was accurately sent and received. Ask something like, "Are you saying . . . ?" before you respond. This clears up about fifty percent of the miscommunications from the start. Remember that you are a team and not competing against each other. Teams win or lose together, and God made husband and wife a team. Be sure to stay on topic, not confusing the issues, and work at understanding and being understood, refraining from name-calling. With these tips, we should be able to better understand each other and even what God wants for us.

If you can't get your point across by talking, agree to write each other letters, or dedicate a legal pad to difficult questions. Write what you want, and then ask your spouse to respond within twenty-four hours. This gives us time and space to process information and avoid overly emotional responses.

Time Out

When we need more time and space to process something that upsets us, agree to call a "time out." A "time out" can be up to two or three days long or as short as twenty minutes. Don't say, "I won't talk about it." Say instead, "I need to calm myself down and will talk about it at a reasonable time." We never want to trap or block each other. Unbridled emotions can do much harm.

Prayer

Some couples and families enjoy praying together; others prefer individual quiet time. This needs to be discovered by the families themselves. Know that each person has a different level of comfort with any given intimate act, such as prayer, so keep the length of time spent praying reasonable for both. Remember that prayers are meant to bring us to a place of quiet where we can be open to hear God's whisper. It is also wise to read Scripture daily, together or individually, allowing God to be close to our minds and allowing us to grow and share together. Be sure to include the children, pray with them, and allow them to see you pray. This is perhaps one of the greatest gifts that we can offer our offspring and is our Christian responsibility as parents. If you are not used to praying, start with the Trisagion Prayers or even the Lord's Prayer; share with God and listen. Many benefit from using a prayer book, while others prefer to pray psalms or their own prayers.

Forgiveness

Christianity is all about new beginnings, and God calls us to undertake new beginnings all the time. He forgives seventy times seven. This is kind of a scriptural code. Seven is the number of fullness, with there being seven days in a week. Seventy is that fullness times ten, and we multiply that everything by everything again. God gives new life, abundant life, and new beginnings. We need to do the same. Forgiveness means that we detach ourselves from the passionate response to the violation or offense. We may remember the offense, but the remembering is passionless, and the memory is treated like data without an emotional response attached to it.

Dates

Dating shouldn't stop with the wedding. Put your best foot forward and make time for each other; get away from your homes and routines, and get some time together. I suggest weekly dates, with husband and wife taking turns planning and organizing them. Later on, when there are children, this will include taking responsibility for finding babysitters.

Meetings

Partners in any relationship need a time deliberately set aside to catch each other up on goings-on and plans for the future. Having a regular, fixed meeting time and place, where both come equipped with notes and calendars, is the best practice. My wife and I would meet at the same restaurant for lunch on Thursdays.[6] Meeting in public places tends to keep things a bit more formal and civil.

Birth Order

There is a lot of information out there about the position and role that birth order plays in influencing how we relate to others. For example, firstborn children are often used to being in charge and taking care of others, while the last-born may be used to being taken care of. While this combination in dating is familiar and therefore comfortable and attractive, after a while one becomes tired of taking care of the other, and the other grows weary of being taken care of. The good news is that if each of you can discover what role you play in the family, you can agree to change it, but this takes planning, being deliberate, and sharing what is changing and why with your partner.

Love You but Not in Love with You

Sociologists talk about two kinds of marital love: intimacy and commitment. No two human beings have the same level of tolerance for intense intimacy, so healthy couples are constantly distancing

---

[6]Another story from Bishop John.

themselves from each other and coming back together, like clapping hands. You couldn't clap without moving your hands apart and then bringing them back together. This is normal and healthy. Sociologists also show that human beings enjoy novelty from early infancy. We like to look at new things. In healthy marriages, the intensity of intimate love seems to decline before leveling off, while committed love increases and then levels off.

Sometimes people say something like, "I love you but am not in love with you." When they say, "I love you," they mean "committed love," and by "not in love with you" they mean the "intimate love" (sexual attraction) that is all about novelty. In other words, this is not unusual and need not be a problem. There is a normal progression of intimate love and committed love. It is the committed love that sustains marriages, and the intimate love is a bonus. Both loves should continue throughout the life of the marriage, and both need our attention.

Saying You Are Sorry

The takeaway line from the movie *Love Story* is "Love means never having to say you are sorry." Fr Thomas Hopko (of blessed memory) said that it would be more true to say love means always having to say you are sorry. The late Dr John Boojamra, former chairman of the Orthodox Christian Education Commission and adjunct professor at St Vladimir's Seminary, encouraged families to treat each other as well as they would a guest in their home. Showing respect to our spouses and children goes a long way in promoting healthy marriages and living peaceful and Christian lives. Christianity is all about respect (fear or awe of God), the love of all other persons, and new beginnings.

Questions for Orthodox Courting or the Newlywed Game

W e would do well to discuss these questions before marriage. When used in a parish setting, it may be fun to set up a forum like the Newlywed Game to explore such issues. Be creative and have fun discovering a bit more about each other.

How many children do you want?

Where do you anticipate celebrating Christmas?

Where will you baptize your children?

Will you homeschool, or use public or private schools?

Is birth control an option?

Will you have separate bank accounts?

Will you ask permission before making major purchases?

Will you have separate vacations?

Will you have nights out with the boys/girls?

Where will you vacation?

Will you save for retirement?

Will you rent or purchase a home?

Will you save before or after paying debts?

Will you buy new or used cars?

Who will do the laundry?

Who will do the cooking?

Will someone stop working to take care of kids?

How much is enough for retirement in today's dollars?

How comfortable are you with debt?

How often will you pray together?

When will you pray?

Where will you go to church?

Abbreviations

ANF = *The Ante-Nicene Fathers*. Edited by Alexander Roberts and James Donaldson. 10 vols. Buffalo, 1885–1896. Reprint, Peabody, MA: Hendrickson, 1994.

NPNF¹ = *The Nicene and Post-Nicene Fathers*, Series 1. Edited by Philip Schaff. New York, 1886–1889. 14 vols. Reprint, Peabody, MA: Hendrickson, 1994.

NPNF² = *The Nicene and Post-Nicene Fathers,* Series 2. Edited by Philip Schaff and Henry Wace. New York, 1890. 14 vols. Reprint, Peabody, MA: Hendrickson, 1994.

LCL = Loeb Classical Library. Cambridge, MA: Harvard University Press.

Bibliography

Augustine of Hippo. *On Marriage and Concupiscence*. NPNF¹ 5:257–308.

_____. *On the Good of Marriage*. NPNF¹ 3:397–413.

_____. *On the Holy Trinity*. NPNF¹ 3:1–228.

Chapman, Gary D. *The Five Love Languages: How to Express Heartfelt Commitment to Your Mate*. Chicago, IL: Northfield, 1995.

Chryssavgis, John. *Love, Sexuality, and the Sacrament of Marriage*. Brookline, MA: Holy Cross Orthodox Press, 1996.

Clement of Alexandria. *The Instructor*. ANF 2:207–98.

Cyril of Jerusalem. *Catechetical Lectures*. NPNF² 7:1–157.

Drower, E. S. *Water Into Wine: A Study of Ritual Idiom in the Middle East*. London: Murray, 1956.

The Great Book of Needs: Expanded and Supplemented. Vol. 1, *The Holy Mysteries*. South Canaan, PA: St. Tikhon's Seminary Press, 2000.

Gregory Nazianzen. *Orations*. NPNF² 7:185–434.

Herodotus. *The Persian Wars*. Translated by A. D. Godley. 4 vols. Loeb Classical Library 117–120. Cambridge, MA: Harvard University Press, 1920–25.

John Chrysostom. *Homilies on 1 Timothy*. NPNF¹ 13:407–73.

_____. *Homilies on Ephesians*. NPNF¹ 13:49–172.

_____. *On Marriage and Family Life*. Translated by Catherine P. Roth and David Anderson. Popular Patristics Series 7. Crestwood, NY: St Vladimir's Seminary Press, 1986.

_____. *Two Homilies on Eutropius. NPNF*[1] 9:243–65.

John of Damascus. *Saint John of Damascus: Writings.* Translated by Frederic Henry Chase, Jr. Vol. 37 of The Fathers of the Church: A New Translation. Washington, DC: Catholic University of America Press, 1958.

Kallistos (Ware). Foreword to *Marriage as a Path to Holiness: Lives of Married Saints,* by David Ford and Mary Ford, ix–xi. 2nd ed. Waymart, PA: St. Tikhon's Monastery Press, 2013.

Kesich, Veselin. "St. Paul: Anti-Feminist or Liberator?" *St Vladimir's Theological Quarterly* 21.3 (1977): 123–47.

The Liturgikon: The Book of Divine Services for the Priest and Deacon. 2nd ed. Englewood, NJ: Antiochian Orthodox Christian Archdiocese of North America, 1989.

Love Story. Directed by Arthur Hiller. Performed by Ali MacGraw and Ryan O'Neal. United States: Paramount Pictures, 1970. Film.

Macarius the Great. *Fifty Spiritual Homilies of St. Macarius the Egyptian.* Translated by Arthur James Mason. Translations of Christian Literature Series I: Greek Text. London: Society For Promoting Christian Knowledge, 1921.

Methodius. *The Symposium: A Treatise on Chastity.* Translated by Herbert Musurillo. Ancient Christian Writers 27. New York: Paulist Press, 1958.

Meyendorff, John. *Marriage: An Orthodox Perspective.* Crestwood, NY: St Vladimir's Seminary Press, 1975.

Najim, Michel. *The Theology of the Orthodox Sacrament of Matrimony and its Implication in our Family Life.*

The Orthodox Study Bible. Nashville, TN: Thomas Nelson, 2008.

Patrinacos, Nicon D. *A Dictionary of Greek Orthodoxy: Lexikon Hellenikes Orthodoxias.* Pleasantville, NY: Hellenic Heritage Publications, 1984.

Prudentius. *Prudentius.* Translated by H. J. Thomson. 2 vols. Loeb Classical Library. Cambridge, MA: Harvard University Press, 1949–53.

Ryken, Leland, James C. Wilhoit, and Tremper Longman III, eds. *Dictionary of Biblical Imagery.* Downers Grove, IL: IVP Academic, 1998.

The Sacrament of Holy Matrimony. With commentary by V. Rev. John Meyendorff. New York, NY: Department of Religious Education of the Orthodox Church in America, 2009.

Schmemann, Alexander. *For the Life of the World: Sacraments and Orthodoxy.* Crestwood, NY: St Vladimir's Seminary Press, 1973.

————. "Liturgical Theology of Marriage." Lecture. St Vladimir's Orthodox Theological Seminary, Crestwood, NY, 1977.

————. *Liturgy and Life: Lectures and Essays on Christian Development through Liturgical Experience.* New York: Department of Religious Education of the Orthodox Church in America, 1974.

————. *Of Water and the Spirit: A Liturgical Study of Baptism.* Crestwood, NY: St Vladimir's Seminary Press, 1974.

————. "Protopresbyter Alexander Schmemann: Forgiveness Sunday." Accessed March 10, 2017. http://www.schmemann.org/byhim/forgivenesssunday.html.

Service Book of the Holy Eastern Orthodox Catholic and Apostolic Church. 8th ed. Englewood, NJ: Antiochian Orthodox Christian Archdiocese of New York and All North America, 1987.

Staniloae, Dumitru. *The World: Creation and Deification.* Edited by Robert Barringer and translated by Ioan Ioniţă. Vol. 2 of The Experience of God. Brookline, MA: Holy Cross Orthodox Press, 1994.

Stevenson, Kenneth. *Nuptial Blessing: A Study of Christian Marriage Rites.* New York: Oxford University Press, 1983.

Tannen, Deborah. *You Just Don't Understand: Women and Men in Conversation.* New York: Ballantine, 1990.

Tertullian. *Apology.* ANF 3:17–60.

_____. *On Exhortation to Chastity.* ANF 4:50–58.

Thayer, Joseph Henry, trans., rev., and enl., C. L. Wilibald Grimm, and C. G. Wilke. *A Greek-English Lexicon of the New Testament: Being Grimm's Wilke's Clavis Novi Testamenti.* 4th ed. 1901; repr., Grand Rapids, MI: Baker Book House, 1977.

Zizioulas, John. *Lessons on Christian Dogmatics.* Thessaloniki: Publication Services, 2005.